A
PROFOUND
MIND

A
PROFOUND
MIND

CULTIVATING WISDOM
IN EVERYDAY LIFE

THE DALAI LAMA

EDITED BY
NICHOLAS VREELAND

THREE RIVERS PRESS
NEW YORK

Published in the United States by Three Rivers Press,
an imprint of the Crown Publishing Group,
a division of Random House, Inc., New York.
www.crownpublishing.com

THREE RIVERS PRESS and the Tugboat design are
registered trademarks of Random House, Inc.

Originally published in hardcover in the United States
by Harmony Books, an imprint of the Crown Publishing Group,
a division of Random House, Inc., New York, in 2011.

Library of Congress Cataloging-in-Publication Data
is available upon request.

ISBN 978-0-385-51468-2
eISBN 978-0-307-95244-8

PRINTED IN THE UNITED STATES OF AMERICA

Book design by Elizabeth Rendfleisch
Cover design by Lloyd&co
Cover photograph: Nicholas Vreeland

3 5 7 9 10 8 6 4

First Paperback Edition

Contents

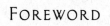

FOREWORD

PERHAPS THE CHIEF difference between Buddhism and the world's other major faith traditions lies in its presentation of our core identity. The existence of the soul or self, which is affirmed in different ways by Hinduism, Judaism, Christianity, and Islam, is not only firmly denied in Buddhism; belief in it is identified as the source of all our misery. The Buddhist path is fundamentally a process of learning to recognize the essential nonexistence of the self, while seeking to help others to recognize it as well.

A mere acknowledgment of the nonexistence of any core self will not free us from our difficulties. We must cultivate a profound mind by deepening our understanding and strengthening it through contemplation and logical study.

And for this profound mind to evolve into the omniscient mind of a Buddha capable of effectively directing others on their paths to enlightenment, it must be motivated by more than a wish for our own peace.

In 2003, Khyongla Rato Rinpoche, founder of Kunkhyab Thardo Ling ("Land Pervaded by

Seekers of Liberation," otherwise known as The Tibet Center), joined with Richard Gere and his charitable organization Healing the Divide to invite His Holiness the Dalai Lama to New York City. They asked the Dalai Lama if he would speak in particular on the Buddhist view of selflessness, as expounded in *Root Verses on Indian Philosophies—The Lion's Roar,* a seventeenth-century Tibetan text by Jamyang Shepa, a scholar distinguished for his knowledge of the different philosophical views extant in India in Buddhism's heyday. In order that His Holiness's lectures include a practical aspect, they also asked that he speak on the meditative technique outlined in *Seven Point Mind Training,* a brief work composed in the twelfth century by the renowned Tibetan practitioner Chekawa Yeshe Dorje.

A few years later, in 2007, Khyongla Rato Rinpoche and Richard Gere again invited His Holiness to New York, this time to present a teaching on the *Diamond Cutter Sutra,* a classic discourse by the Buddha on the emptiness of inherent existence of all that exists. The Dalai Lama also included in this visit an exposition on *Seventy Verses on Emptiness,* by Nagarjuna, the second-century Buddhist philosopher considered by many to be the greatest single explicator of the Buddha's often challenging and seemingly paradoxical teachings on emptiness.

Throughout all these talks His Holiness sought not only to

lead his listeners through the complexities of the Buddhist doctrine of selflessness, but to show them how to bring these teachings actively into their own lives. It is by actually living these teachings that we allow them to bring about a genuine transformation in our perception of ourselves and our lives.

This book comes out of those talks, all wonderfully translated by Geshe Thupten Jinpa. It is offered in the earnest hope that it may further the understanding in the West of the Buddhist doctrine of selflessness and its usefulness in living a more meaningful and happy life.

I would like to extend my profound thanks to all those who have helped me in the preparation of this volume, and to assure the reader that any errors he or she may find within are purely my own.

Nicholas Vreeland

INTRODUCTION

IT IS MY hope that in this book we can explore the true beliefs of Buddhism so that misconceptions might be dispelled. I also hope that for those of you who are practitioners of another religion, this book might help you come to understand the beliefs of a fellow religious tradition. If there is anything you wish to incorporate into your practice, I hope that you will do so.

We will look at some of the philosophical interpretations of the teachings of Lord Buddha over 2,500 years ago and will examine topics such as emptiness and dependent origination. We will then discuss how to cultivate these as well as the altruistic mind of enlightenment that in Sanskrit we call Bodhicitta.

As we progress, we must apply what we learn. There is a Tibetan saying that there should be no gap so large between our mental state and what is being taught that we could fall through it. As you read, I hope that you will relate what you are hearing to your own personal experience; as I teach, I try to do the same.

If the material that I am trying to impart

remains opaque to me, how can I possibly convey its meaning to others? Though I can't claim to have great mastery of the subjects we are discussing here, with subject matter as important as I feel this is, even a mediocre understanding is much better than none at all. However, as a result of your reading a book that stems from my mediocre understanding, you can only hope to gain an understanding that will be half knowledge and half ignorance. But this, too, is much better than no understanding at all!

CHAPTER 1

Diverse Spiritual Traditions

BUDDHISTS BELIEVE THAT we are responsible for the quality of our lives, our happiness, and our resources. In order to achieve a meaningful life we must transform our own emotions, as this is the most effective way to bring about future happiness for ourselves and for all others.

No one can force us to transform our minds, not even the Buddha. We must do so voluntarily. Therefore Buddha stated, "You are your own master."

Our efforts must be realistic. We must establish for ourselves that the methods we are following will bring about our desired results. We can't merely rely on faith. It is essential that we scrutinize the path we intend to follow to establish clearly what is and what is not effective, so that the methods of our efforts may succeed. This, I believe, is essential if we wish to find any true happiness in life.

I hesitate to tell you about a spiritual tradition that is not your own. There exist many fine religions that have, over centuries, helped their followers attain peace of mind and happiness.

There may, however, be aspects of Buddhism that you could bring to your spiritual practice.

Also, some of you have put your religion aside and are looking elsewhere for answers to your deeper inquiries. You may have an inclination toward Eastern philosophies with their belief in karma and past lives. A few young Tibetans have similarly discarded their Buddhist origins, finding spiritual solace in Christianity and Islam.

Unfortunately many of us from the various traditions of Buddhism, including Chinese, Japanese, Thai, and Sri Lankan, simply call ourselves Buddhists without really knowing the meaning of Buddha's word. Nagarjuna, one of Buddhism's greatest scholars and practitioners, wrote many explanatory works on Buddhist thought and practice that reflect the need to know Buddha's teaching well. In order to develop our understanding we must study those teachings. If deep understanding were not so crucial to our practice of Buddhism, I doubt that the great scholars of the past would have bothered to write their important treatises.

Many misconceptions about Buddhism have arisen, particularly around Tibetan Buddhism, which is often depicted as mysterious and esoteric, involving the worship of wrathful, bloodthirsty deities. I think that we Tibetans, with our fondness for ornate ceremonies and elaborate costumes, are partly responsible for this. Though much of the ritual of our practice has come to us from Buddha himself, we are surely guilty of some embellishment. Maybe the cold climate of Tibet became a justification for our sartorial excesses. Tibetan lamas—our teachers—are also responsible for misconceptions. Each little village had its own monastery with a resident lama who presided over local society. This tradition has mistakenly become identified as Lamaism, suggesting that ours is a separate religion from Buddhism.

In this time of globalization it seems to me particularly important that we familiarize ourselves with the beliefs of others. The great cities of the West, with their multicultural flavor, have become veritable microcosms of our planet. All the world religions live side by side here. For there to be harmony between these communities it is essential that we know about each other's beliefs.

Why is it that there are such diverse philosophies with so many varied spiritual traditions based upon them? From the Buddhist point of view we recognize the great diversity in the mental inclinations and dispositions of human beings. Not only are we humans all so very different from one another, but our tendencies—which Buddhists consider to be inherited from past lives—vary greatly as well. Given the diversity this implies, it is understandable that we find such a vast spectrum of philosophical systems and spiritual traditions. These are an important heritage of mankind, serving human needs. We must appreciate the value of philosophical and spiritual diversity.

Even within the teachings of Buddha Shakyamuni we find a variety of philosophical positions. There are times when Buddha explicitly states that the physical and mental parts that constitute each of us can be likened to a burden carried by a person, suggesting that the person exists as an autonomous self—"me"—possessing and ruling over "my" parts. In other teachings the Buddha refutes any objective existence at all. We accept the diversity of the Buddha's teachings as a reflection of his skillful ability to address the great variety of mental inclinations of his diverse followers.

When we examine the spiritual traditions extant in the world, we find that all agree on the importance of ethical practice. Even the ancient Indian Charvakas—nihilists who denied any kind of afterlife—stated that since this is our only life, it is important to lead it morally, by disciplining our minds and trying to better ourselves.

All spiritual traditions aim to overcome our temporary and long-term suffering and to achieve lasting happiness. No religion seeks to increase our misery. We find compassion and wisdom to be fundamental qualities of God described in the various theistic traditions. In no faith tradition is the divinity conceived as the embodiment of hatred or hostility. This is because compassion and wisdom are qualities that we humans naturally and spontaneously regard as virtuous. Intuiting these qualities as desirable, we naturally project them onto our conceptions of the divine.

I believe that if we are truly devoted to God, our love for God will necessarily be expressed in our daily behavior, particularly in the way we treat others. To behave otherwise would render one's love for God futile.

When I spoke at an interfaith memorial service at the National Cathedral in Washington, DC, in September of 2003 to commemorate the victims of the tragedy suffered on September 11, 2001, I felt it important to express my fear that some might view Islam as a belligerent religion. I warned that this would be a grave mistake because, at its core, Islam has the same ethical values as all the other great world faith traditions, with a particular emphasis on kindheartedness toward others. I have always been impressed with Islam's attention to social justice, especially its prohibition of financial exploitation through charging interest and its injunction against intoxicants. According to my Muslim friends, there is no way for a true practitioner of Islam to justify inflicting harm on another human being. They emphasize that anyone who harms a fellow human being in the name of Islam is not a proper Muslim. It is important to ensure that we not fall into the temptation of criticizing Islam for the faults of individuals who have so misrepresented one of the world's great religions.

It heartens me to have met devoted Christian monks and nuns, as well as Jewish rabbis, who, while remaining profoundly faithful to their religious tradition, have adopted certain Buddhist practices they find beneficial. When Shakyamuni Buddha first taught Buddhism, introducing a new philosophy and spiritual practice to the world 2,500 years ago, it was not without incorporating helpful elements that had their origins elsewhere. In doing so he included many existing beliefs and practices, such as the acceptance of past lives and the cultivation of a single-pointed mind.

In our quest to learn more about other faiths and the ideas they hold, it is important that we remain true to our own faith. In my opinion it is much safer and wiser to remain within one's own faith tradition, as we often become overly excited about a new possession, only to become dissatisfied with it later. There is a danger that we approach our initial interest in Buddhism with the enthusiasm of a novice and then become disenchanted. On my first visit to India, in 1956, I met a European Buddhist nun who seemed particularly devoted to her practice of her newly adopted religion. After returning to India as a refugee in 1959, I asked about this person and was told that though she had initially been fervent in her practice, upon returning to her home country she had become extremely critical of Buddhism.

I also remember a Polish woman who had become a member of the Theosophical Society in Madras in the 1940s. She was very helpful to my fellow Tibetans in setting up an education system for our refugee children. She became deeply interested in Buddhism and at some point appeared to have become a Buddhist. Later in her life, however, when she was in her eighties and approaching the critical time of her death, the concept of a creator being seemed to consume her, causing her much confusion. I therefore advised her to think of God, to feel love for God, and to pray to her idea of God. It is for this reason that I stress the importance of keeping to our own traditions. Changing religions without seriously analyzing what we are adopting will not lead to the happiness we all seek.

WHAT IS THE MEANING OF LIFE?

Though wealth may be important to our happiness, I do not believe that it is supremely so. Mere wealth fails to bring us deep inner satisfaction. We are all aware of the unhappiness that often accompanies affluence. I also believe that good companions are secondary. Though a spouse may provide temporary solace from the pains of life, I don't think that family and friends can ultimately provide the true inner happiness we seek. Loved ones often bring more anxiety to our lives, while a calm and peaceful mind imparts a profound happiness that can even affect our physical state.

An intelligent mind, with a certain quality of calm and compassion, has the potential to be developed into a truly peaceful mind, one that brings happiness to us and to those around us. How can we bring about a calm, peaceful mind? Intoxicants are not the answer. We may think that simpleminded animals have the solution, but their mental state is limited and cannot be further enhanced.

I consider compassion to be a mental quality that can bring us true lasting inner peace and inner strength. We cultivate it by using our intelligence to transform our emotions. We reduce our selfishly induced destructive emotions and increase our selfless constructive ones, bringing about happiness within ourselves and others.

We are born with a basic potential for compassion that is essential for our continued existence. Though emotions such as fear and hatred can also be vital to our survival, our sophisticated minds are easily swayed by a false confidence that anger can instill in us. We neglect our more positive emotions and overlook our sense of respect for others, our civic responsibilities, or our wish to share others' problems. With such false feelings of independence we feel that we have no need for others. This inflated sense of self leads away from the inner peace and happiness we seek and affects those around us in an equally negative way.

THE BUDDHIST NOTION OF SELF

Humanity has evolved various faith traditions, some of which believe in a creator being—a God—and others do not. Of the nontheistic religions, only Buddhism and Jainism are still practiced today. Though the ancient Indian Samkya philosophy had both a theistic branch that believed in Brahma, the creator, and a nontheistic division, I haven't met any of its adherents, and wonder whether any still exist.

Among these three nontheistic views, the Jains and nontheistic Samkyas propound an independent self or "I," which they call *atman*. The existence of this independent self is denied by Buddhists. The differentiation between Buddhist and non-Buddhist philosophical schools of ancient India is therefore determined by whether or not an eternal, enduring, permanent self is accepted.

Though in Buddhism we do speak of a self, we hold any

concept of "I" to be merely designated, or identified, in dependence on the body and mind that make us up.

All of the three nontheistic views share a conviction in the law of causality—karma—that is responsible for all that might otherwise be attributed to a creator.

DEPENDENT ORIGINATION

A radical difference that exists between Buddhists and non-Buddhists concerns the principle of dependent origination—*pratityasamutpada*. On a coarse level, dependent origination refers simply to something's dependence on causes and conditions, and explains the origination of everything in terms of cause and effect. It is due to dependent origination, for example, that spiritual practice is effective and brings about inner changes. According to Buddhists, such changes do not happen due to God's wish; instead they happen as a result of our implementation of proper causes. This is why Buddha stated that we are our own masters. Given that our future well-being is in our own hands, it is we—by our own behavior—who determine whether or not our future will be happy.

CHAPTER 2

WHAT IS DISTINCT ABOUT BUDDHISM

BUDDHISM CAN BE distinguished from other faith traditions and philosophical schools by four "seals." These are the marks or characteristics of Buddhism.

The first of these states that all conditioned things are impermanent and transient. This is something we know intimately as we watch ourselves grow older. We can also see reflections of impermanence in the physical world around us as it changes from day to day, from season to season, and from year to year.

Impermanence is not limited to the eventual wearing out and disintegration of things; it can be subtler than this. Things exist only momentarily, each moment of their existence causing the next, which then in turn causes the next. Let's take an apple. For the first day or two it may remain quite similar in appearance and ripeness to the apple we initially consider. Over time, however, it will get riper and riper, and eventually rot. If we leave it out long enough, it will disintegrate into something that we no longer identify as an apple. Eventually, when it has decomposed totally, there will be no apple at all. This is a manifestation of the grosser aspect of impermanence.

On a more subtle level, the apple changes from moment to moment, each moment serving as the cause of the next. As we recognize this momentary nature of the apple, it becomes difficult to claim that there is an underlying apple possessing these moments of its existence.

This transient quality is also a characteristic of ourselves. We exist momentarily, each moment causing our next moment of existence, which then causes the next moment, a process that proceeds from day to day, month to month, year to year, and maybe even lifetime to lifetime.

This is also true of our environment. Even the most seemingly concrete and enduring objects surrounding us, such as mountains and valleys, change over time—millions of years—and will eventually disappear. Such grosser transformation is only possible because of the constant process of change occurring moment by moment. If there were no such momentary change, there could be no great changes over an extended length of time.

The seventh-century Buddhist logician Dharmakirti stated that "all phenomena arising from causes and conditions are naturally impermanent." This suggests that whatever has come into being due to the aggregation of various causes and conditions is by its very nature subject to change. What is it that brings about this change? We Buddhists hold that the very causes that brought something into being in the first place are responsible for its evolution. Therefore we say that things are under the power of other causes and conditions—they are other-powered.

Some Buddhist thinkers accept the impermanence of our apple to be merely that it comes into being, endures, and then decays, finally ceasing to exist altogether. Most Buddhists understand the apple's impermanence to be its momentary nature: its existence moment by moment by moment, with each moment of our apple ending as the next moment begins. They would consider that the very causes and conditions that bring our apple into being—the apple seed that grew into the apple tree from which our apple was picked, the earth in which the tree grew, the rain that irrigated the tree, the sunshine and fertilizer that nurtured the growth of the seed into a tree—are the same causes and conditions that bring about our apple's disintegration, no other cause being necessary.

What are the causes and conditions of our own individual existence—yours and mine? Our present moment of existence is caused by its immediately preceding moment, going back to the moment of our birth, and further back, through the nine months in our mother's womb, to the moment of conception. It is at conception that our physical bodies are caused by the union of our father's semen and our mother's egg. It is also at conception that, according to Buddhism, our mental aspect or consciousness—not being physical—is caused by the previous moment of that consciousness, the momentary stream of which goes back through the experiences between lifetimes, to our past life and to the life before that, and to the life before that, over infinite lives.

The root cause of our unenlightened existence within this cycle of rebirths—*samsara* in Sanskrit—is said to be our fundamental ignorance: our grasping at a sense of self. The views of different Buddhists on this self-grasping ignorance will be explored throughout this book. It is an essential subject, as Buddhism understands its removal to be the way to our true peace and happiness.

We must also initially identify the causes and conditions that shape our unenlightened existence in samsara. These are our afflictive mental attitudes such as craving, aversion, pride, and jealousy. They are afflictive in that they bring about our unhappiness.

Our craving causes us to wish for more and to be unsatisfied with what we have. We are subsequently reborn in a situation of need and dissatisfaction. Aversion diminishes our patience and increases our tendency toward anger. Similarly, all our afflictions—our pride, our jealousy—undermine our peace of mind and cause us to be unhappy.

Such mental afflictions have dominated our actions over infinite past lives. Consequently, our conditioned existence is described as a contaminated reality in that our thoughts are contaminated by afflictive emotions. So long as we are under the influence of these emotions, we are not in control of our selves; we are not truly free. Our existence is therefore fundamentally unsatisfactory, possessing the nature of suffering.

Soon after attaining enlightenment, Shakyamuni Buddha taught about suffering. He identified suffering as divided into three levels. The first and most immediately evident level of suffering is that of mental and physical pain. The second, subtler level of suffering is that which is created not by painful sensations but by pleasurable ones. Why does pleasure cause suffering? Because it always eventually ceases, leaving us anxious for more. But the most important level of suffering is the third, a form of suffering that pervades the whole of our lives. It is this last level of suffering that is referred to in the second characteristic that defines Buddhism: all contaminated phenomena—all things that exist—are bound up in the nature of suffering.

The third of the four characteristics or seals of Buddhism is that all phenomena are devoid of selfhood. Throughout this book we shall discover what is meant by selfhood and the lack thereof.

To review these three first characteristics, all compounded things, be they air, stone, or living creatures, are impermanent, they are in the nature of suffering, and all phenomena are selfless. Our ignorance of this selfless nature of all that exists is the fundamental cause of our unenlightened existence. Fortunately, it is due to this selfless nature that we have the potential for ending our miserable situation in cyclic existence.

The force of wisdom, cultivated gradually, enables us to diminish and eventually eliminate our fundamental ignorance that grasps at a sense of self. The cultivation of wisdom will bring about a state beyond sorrow—*nirvana* in Sanskrit. The fourth characteristic of Buddhism is that nirvana is true peace.

So . . . the root of our unhappiness is our falsely held view that we possess any true or enduring substantial reality. But, says Buddhism, there is a way out of this dilemma. It lies in recognizing our true identity: the one that lies beneath our falsely held conceptions of an enduring personal self.

Our mind is essentially pure and luminous. The afflictive thoughts and emotions that pollute our everyday, surface selves cannot touch this essential mind. Being adventitious, these pollutions are removable. Buddhist practice is aimed primarily at cultivating the antidotes to these afflictive thoughts and emotions, with the goal of eradicating the root of our unenlightened existence to bring about liberation from suffering.

The technique we employ to do this is meditation. There are, of course, several varieties of meditation, and many of these are widely practiced today. The form of meditation we shall focus on in this book differs, however, from a number of these methods in that it is not merely an exercise for calming the mind. Diligent study and contemplation is essential. We familiarize our minds with new ideas, such as ones we are exploring in this book, analyzing them logically, broadening our understanding and deepening our insight. We call this analytical meditation. It is the form of meditation that must be applied to the content of this book if we wish to bring about true change to our perception of ourselves and of our world.

CHAPTER 3

THE BUDDHIST SCHOOLS—
DIVISIONS IN BUDDHISM

WE OFTEN DIVIDE Buddhism into Hinayana and Mahayana, or the Lesser and Greater Vehicles. The Hinayana, or Lesser Vehicle, is directed toward freedom from the misery of life in the cycle of rebirths within which we all find ourselves. The Hinayana practitioner pursues his or her liberation from within the fetters of samsara. Mahayana, meaning Greater Vehicle, refers to a process aimed at attaining Buddhahood, the ultimate enlightened state of omniscience. The Mahayanist endeavors to attain that ultimate state of enlightenment in order to help all others out of their misery as well.

A third vehicle is sometimes distinguished. The Vajrayana or Tantric vehicle is practiced through the repetition of mantras along with advanced methods of visualization and concentration by which one cultivates a particularly subtle state of consciousness that enables quicker progress along the path to full enlightenment. However, as Vajrayana meditative techniques are aimed at the attainment of Buddhahood for the sake of all sentient beings—the myriad variety of possessors of consciousness and a sense of self, which would include people and animals—this vehicle is actually contained within the Mahayana.

Regrettably, Tibetan Buddhist texts often take a reader's familiarity with Buddhism for granted. Traditional Buddhist writings assume that a practitioner is familiar with the idea of karma—the laws of cause and effect—and emptiness. Only through familiarity with these subjects is one able to truly relate from a Buddhist perspective to such topics as the preciousness of human life, the inevitability of death, and the relative nature of all worldly knowledge. Without this contextual knowledge, the effectiveness of our meditation on these subjects will be limited. This is particularly true regarding the practice of Vajrayana. We cannot expect results from Tantric initiations and a daily Tantric practice without firm knowledge of why we are practicing. Many Tibetan and Chinese Buddhists spend a lot of time reciting mantras and chanting prayers without doing much thinking. I doubt that this is very beneficial. Effective Buddhist practice depends upon our understanding of Buddhist doctrines. Without it, we cannot be true Buddhist practitioners.

An alternate division is made between Mahayana and Hinayana based on philosophical tenets. Of the four Buddhist schools of philosophy that we shall be looking at in this book—Vaibhashika, Sautrantika, Cittamatra, and Madhyamika—the first two are lesser or Hinayana, while the latter two are Mahayana.

These two distinct ways of differentiating between Hinayana and Mahayana, on the basis of motivation and philosophical view, lead to a variety of possibilities between the two categories. A Buddhist practitioner might possess the great love and compassion for all sentient beings that would lead him or her to seek Buddhahood in order to best serve others. Such an attitude would define the practitioner as a Bodhisattva—a possessor of Bodhicitta, the altruistic mind of enlightenment, and would establish him or her as a Mahayanist. If, however, this Mahayanist were to hold the philosophical views of the Vaibhashika or Sautrantika, who believe that though we are impermanent, changing moment by moment, there is at the core of each of us a truly existent self possessing mental and physical parts, then he or she would be a holder of Hinayana tenets.

Alternatively, someone might hold the view of the Mahayana's Madhyamika school of philosophy, that all phenomena are empty of even the slightest quality of objective existence, while pursuing a spiritual practice with the Hinayana goal of mere peace from the ever-recurring misery of cyclic existence.

It is therefore our motivation that determines whether we are Hinayanists, out to save ourselves, or Mahayanists, striving to help all sentient beings. And quite separately from whether our motivation is Hinayanist or Mahayanist, we can hold the philo-sophical views of any of the four schools of Buddhist philosophy.

SELFLESSNESS

The view of selflessness is the essence of Buddha's teaching. Buddhist philosophers have interpreted selflessness in different ways. They have sliced away the untenable aspects of self, while attempting not to negate the existence of things altogether. As a result we have an array of views of selflessness that vary from a denial of permanence to a rejection of inherent existence. For the former, the impermanent and momentary quality of a person would be his or her selflessness, while, for others, selflessness would be defined by a person's lack of inherent existence. We may think of the different interpretations of selflessness as rungs of a ladder leading to the ultimate view. Each rung of this ladder helps us recognize subtler aspects of existence—in particular, of how we and the world around us can, and cannot, be said to exist.

What are these different interpretations? Starting from the bottom of the ladder we have the two Hinayana views: the Vaibhashika and Sautrantika schools of philosophy. For both of these, a person may be defined by selflessness, but all other phenomena—such as the physical and mental parts that a person is made up of—are not. Their understanding of selflessness focuses on a person's lack of self-sufficiency and independence. A follower of one of these schools attempts to recognize this specifically dependent quality of his or her existence.

The philosophers of the higher rungs of the ladder, those of the Cittamatra or "Mind-Only" school, and the subtler Madhyamika or "Middle Way" school, argue that such a definition of selflessness is too restricted. These Mahayana philosophers have extended the concept of selflessness to encompass the parts that make up a person: the physical as well as mental aggregates that constitute our existence. They contend that the notion of selflessness must extend to include everything within existence. They further argue that as long as there is some quality of self or attribution of any inherent existence to an object, there will remain the potential for our eventually feeling attachment or aversion for it.

Mind-Only

We may accept the idea that there is no self that is separate from, and independent of, the parts that make us up. But how do we then apply this same quality of selflessness to the things that make up the world around us? The Mind-Only school suggests that objects seem to naturally be the points of reference of our thoughts and of the terms that we apply to them. A house appears to be the basis for our naming it "house," suggesting that among the walls, the roof, and the foundation there is something that naturally warrants the composite of those parts being identified as "house." There is, however, nothing in the house or among its parts that can establish it to be the natural candidate for the term "house." The house's basis for being called "house" is purely conventional. English speakers agree that a particular assembly of wood, nails, and plaster is referred to as a "house."

Mind-Only philosophers go on to propose that our perception of outside objects—tables and chairs, for example—is but the maturing of potentials. A table is perceived not because it exists in the room before me, but because some potential within the continuum of beginningless moments of my mind has ripened and manifested. The table I see is therefore not separate from my perception of it; it is actually of one nature with my mind's perception of it. The name Mind-Only refers to the nondual nature of subject and object—the mind and its perceiving object.

This non-separateness of the mind and its object is how Mind-Only philosophers apply selflessness to phenomena as well as persons. However, in the process they seem to attribute the existence of all outer phenomena to the mind perceiving them, investing the mind with a quality of existence that is challenged by the philosophers on the next rung of the ladder.

Middle Way

The Middle Way or Madhyamika philosophers contend that self-lessness as applied to a person and to the things a person experiences must be applied to the person's mind as well: to his or her feelings, thoughts, emotions, experiences, and consciousness itself. Just as an independently existent chair cannot be found among its parts, so the mind cannot be found among the feelings and emotions that comprise it.

Madhyamika philosophers go so far as to question the very notion of objective or inherent existence of things. Nagarjuna, the Madhyamika trailblazer of the second century CE, points out that if any quality of objective existence is attributed to a thing, no matter how subtle that quality may be, it becomes the basis for the occurrence of afflictions and their ensuing suffering.

To deny some intrinsic quality of existence of a thing would seem to be a negation of the thing itself. Buddhist philosophers of the lower rungs, such as Dharmakirti, state that every phenomenon must possess its own defining characteristic. This suggests that on a fundamental level things need to have some intrinsic reality in order to exist. How can a chair be free of inherent chair-ness? It would seem absurd. However, it is just this quality of existence that the Madhyamika philosophers are refuting.

Nagarjuna explains that by refuting inherent existence he is not denying existence per se. What's more, he suggests that it is precisely due to this lack of inherent existence that phenomena can exist at all. Our perception of a chair as possessing its own inherent chair-ness is illusory. It is based on the incorrect assumption that the chair exists in its own right as the bearer of the name "chair." A chair can only exist because of its lack or emptiness of any inherent existence. That emptiness of chair-ness is what makes the existence of a chair possible.

To recap, we can see how the lines of logical reasoning put forward by the different Buddhist philosophical schools to establish how things can exist become more and more subtle as we go up the rungs of our philosophical ladder. Phenomena are initially understood to depend on causes and conditions, and are thereby seen to lack independent autonomous existence. They are then seen to exist as manifestations of inner potencies, and thus not to be independent of the mind experiencing them. Ultimately, phenomena are thought to exist as mere names or designations, lacking even their own inherent existence.

As has been said, according to Nagarjuna's interpretation of selflessness, there can be no difference between the selflessness of a person and the selflessness of phenomena. The person or "I" cannot be found within the physical or mental elements that make him or her up, nor is the person found to be either the collection or the continuum of those physical and mental elements. Our sense of "I" is thus found to be nothing more than a construct or an idea applied to the physical and mental aggregates or parts that serve as the basis for such a designation. Similarly, each of the phenomena of which we are composed exists merely as a concept based upon its own aggregates. And the same is true of the parts of which those aggregates are composed.

According to the philosophical schools of the lower rungs of our ladder, a realization of one's lack of substantially existent self-sufficiency is all that is necessary to attain freedom from cyclic existence. The ultimate attainment of Buddhahood, however, necessitates a realization of the view that all phenomena—including ourselves—are empty of self. In accordance with the view put forward by Shakyamuni Buddha in his Perfection of Wisdom Sutras, Nagarjuna's Madhyamika school holds that in order to extricate oneself from the torment of samsara, the same view of selflessness must be realized as that which a Bodhisattva cultivates in his or her pursuit of the omniscient state of Buddhahood.

The Buddha states in the Perfection of Wisdom Sutras:

*Those wishing to follow the path of Listeners must train in the
    Perfection of Wisdom;*
*Those wishing to pursue the path of Solitary-Realizers must also
    train in the Perfection of Wisdom;*
*And those wishing to engage in the path of Bodhisattvas, too
    must train in the Perfection of Wisdom.*

Listeners and Solitary-Realizers have attained freedom from
samsara in accord with Hinayana aspirations. Bodhisattvas aspire to attain the ultimate freedom of Buddhahood. All must
train in the perfection of wisdom in the sense that they must perfect their realization of selflessness.

CHAPTER 4

THE FOUR NOBLE TRUTHS

TO CHANGE OUR lives we must first acknowledge that our present situation is not satisfactory. Any desire to pursue a spiritual path of inner transformation will arise only when we recognize the underlying miserable state we're in. Were we content and happy with our lives, there would be little reason to seek change. The Buddha therefore initially taught the first noble truth, establishing suffering as the actual state of our existence.

Our acknowledgment of the unhappy predicament we find ourselves in will naturally lead us to ask what has brought this condition about. The second noble truth explains the origin of our suffering state. According to the Buddhist view, our misery in cyclic existence is caused by our afflictive emotions provoking us to behave selfishly. Our self-centered acts in turn cause us unhappiness and a tendency to repeat our nonvirtuous behavior, thereby producing more misery. This tragic series of events, drawn out over many lifetimes and provoking ever greater suffering, is all caused by actions on our part that derive from our grasping at a notion of "me" at the core of our being. From this self-grasping ensues the self-cherishing that motivates us to satisfy ourselves in all possible manners and to protect ourselves from any challenge to our happiness. Our misery is thus seen to originate from causes—physical, verbal, and particularly mental actions perpetrated by us—that stem from our grasping at a core self.

Were we to realize that this self did not actually exist, our recognition would naturally inhibit selfish behavior, and our instinctive tendency to act in ways that cause us future misery would thereby cease. In the third noble truth, the Buddha taught that all suffering ends when we bring about a cessation of its causes.

Our tendency to grasp at a sense of self, and to cherish that self, is a habit deeply instilled in the fiber of our being. To bring about any change in such habitual behavior demands a process of training over many years. To end our involvement in samsara altogether will take numerous lifetimes of practice. In the fourth noble truth the Buddha taught how we must engage in the training leading to liberation from samsara.

The Buddha actually taught the Four Noble Truths from three different perspectives. He initially identified the individual truths, stating:

This is the truth of suffering;
These are true origins (of suffering);
This is true cessation (of suffering);
This is the true path to cessation.

In the second set of statements the Buddha established a system by which the knowledge of the Four Noble Truths can be implemented into one's practice. He stated:

Suffering is to be recognized,
Its origins eliminated;
Cessation must be actualized,
And the path cultivated.

The third set of statements reflects the ultimate nature of the Four Noble Truths: their emptiness of any inherent existence. A more practical interpretation might be that the Buddha was presenting the consequence of our implementing the Four Noble Truths. By internalizing our knowledge of the Four Noble Truths we can overcome suffering to the extent that it is no more; we can eliminate the origins of suffering so that there is nothing to eliminate; we can actualize cessation so that there is no cessation; and we can cultivate the path to the point that there is no longer a path to cultivate. The Buddha stated:

> *Although suffering is to be recognized, there is no suffering to recognize;*
> *Although its origin is to be overcome, there is no origin to overcome;*
> *Although cessation must be actualized, there is no cessation to actualize;*
> *Although the path must be cultivated, there is no path to cultivate.*

As I have mentioned, a Buddhist practitioner aspires to attain freedom from samsaric misery by eliminating its root cause, our fundamental ignorance of the lack of inherent existence in everything we perceive. We are bound in cyclic existence by this ignorance as it impels the other afflictions such as attachment, anger, pride, and jealousy. It is this bondage by our afflictions that we seek to end.

The cessation of our misery is the true Buddhist meaning of the Sanskrit word *Dharma*. Dharma often denotes scriptures that represent Buddha's speech and contain his doctrine. Dharma can also refer to phenomena—all that exists. However, the most important meaning of the term is liberation from all suffering. Our pursuit of this peaceful state of nirvana is a quest for protection from the misery of samsara, and particularly from the afflictions such as attachment and aversion that bind us within the vicious cycle of rebirths. Hence, when as Buddhists we "take refuge in the Dharma" we do so in pursuit of protection from our wretched plight. The Dharma is therefore seen to represent nirvana, the state of freedom from samsaric suffering. Nirvana itself is the cessation of suffering.

CHAPTER 5

THE ROLE OF KARMA

WHAT CAUSES MENTAL and physical phenomena to be transient and subject to change?
Everything made up of physical or temporal
parts is naturally transient. Similarly, the relationship between causes and their effects is
natural. It's just the way things are. The fact
that consciousness has a quality of clarity and
knowing, or that shapes and colors are visible
forms, is not a result of karma; it's a natural
characteristic of the mechanics of causes and
conditions and dependent origination.

Within the world of dependent origination
there are causes and conditions that relate to
our experience of pain and pleasure. These arise
from karma. Correctly translated as "action,"
karma refers to an act engaged in with intent.
The quality of our intention—itself a mental
action or karma—determines the quality of the
physical action it motivates, thereby establishing the quality of the resultant experience of the
pleasure or pain we undergo. The role of karma
is therefore understood in relation to our experience of suffering and happiness.

Just as we naturally experience feelings of pain and pleasure, we also have an innate sense of "I" toward which we instinctively feel affection. It is because of the affection we hold for ourselves that we feel fondness and love for those around us; our self-affection is the source of the compassion we feel for others. As human beings born from a womb, we are naturally connected to our mother, whose milk we survive on and whose care we are supported by. Our affection for her is an extension of our affection for ourselves. This love has a biological basis, as our survival depends on it. The intimate bond between a mother and her child is not something imposed by society—it is spontaneous. Its intensity is not something that needs to be developed, as a mother derives joy from her selfless devotion to her child.

Other emotions help us survive as well. Attachment is the primary emotion in provoking the conditions that enable our survival, but the emotions of anger and fear play an important part as well. A scientist once told me that the muscles in our arms become stronger when we get angry, enabling us to physically accomplish our anger's purpose. Fear, he told me, causes blood to flow to the muscles in our legs, enabling us to run.

Just as the love that exists between a mother and a child is mixed with attachment, so too is the love we feel for the others who are closest to us. However, just because such emotions have a component of selfishness doesn't mean that they can't serve as the seed from which to develop compassion toward all sentient beings. Self*ish*ness, in other words, can be necessary to survival, but so can self*less*ness. We must contemplate the benefits of selfless love and compassion to our own physical health and to our mental happiness. We must also recognize how this altruistic attitude helps us nurture a happier home environment while also contributing to a healthier and more stable society. It is by means of such contemplation that our appreciation for the value of compassion will strengthen and expand its sphere to encompass more and more beings.

We also deepen our compassion by considering ever subtler levels of suffering. We initially desire that sentient beings be free of the evident physical and emotional pain we call "suffering of suffering." We must also wish that they be separated from the suffering of change—the happy moments that eventually end, causing misery. Most profound is a desire that all sentient beings be free of the pervasive suffering of our conditioned existence within samsara.

Our compassion is also intensified when it is combined with the recognition that suffering is the result of our afflicted states of mind and the karma or actions they provoke, all rooted in the fundamental ignorance of our grasping at a sense of self. With such insight into selflessness we see that this fundamental igno-rance can be rectified and that the cause of suffering can thereby be uprooted. The awareness that sentient beings' suffering can be ended will greatly intensify our compassion for them, turning it from mere pity into active engagement in an attainable goal. This is the approach of a sharp-minded practitioner. It leads to recognition that there is validity in the compassionate path we have undertaken, as its goal is achievable.

SUFFERING AND HAPPINESS

We are each the center of our own universe. We establish east, west, north, and south, as well as up and down, all in relation to our own location. The self can be seen as the fundamental framework by which we understand and relate to the whole of existence.

Suffering, which we can think of as our own individual sam-sara, and happiness, which is our freedom from that suffering, stem ultimately from our notion of self. My suffering results from my indulgence in self-centered behavior. And that behav-ior propels me to act in ways that cause me more suffering. I seem to go round and round within the cycle of rebirths which constitute my samsara. My pursuit of happiness arises from my wish to be free of suffering.

The whole of samsara and nirvana can be viewed in relation to our own individual notion of self. Buddha's teachings on suffering, its causes, the state of cessation from suffering, and the path leading to that state of cessation are all to be considered from the point of view of the individual who, upon recognizing his or her state of suffering, acknowledges the causes of that suffering and works toward ending it by following the path to that cessation. Similarly, religious practices of all faith traditions only make sense when related to the individual engaging in practice.

Buddha has stated that the thought "I am" is the mind of a demon. This is because our mistaken notion of ourselves causes the self-cherishing that lies at the root of all our misery. Buddha has also taught that we are our own masters. Though our present situation within samsara may be the result of our own past karma motivated by afflictions, we have the possibility of generating new virtuous karma in the form of altruistically motivated actions. Our future is in our hands.

CHAPTER 6

IDENTIFYING THE SELF

THE SUFFERING AND happiness that each of us experiences is a reflection of the level of distortion or clarity with which we view ourselves and the world. To know and experience the nature of self correctly is to experience nirvana. To know the nature of self in a distorted manner is to experience samsara. It is therefore imperative that we devote ourselves to establishing just what the nature of self is!

In Dharmakirti's *Pramanavartika* (Exposition of Valid Cognition), he states:

When there is grasping at self,
Discrimination between self and others arises;
Emotions and afflictions then follow.

If we observe our perceptions and thoughts we notice that a sense of self arises in us very naturally. We instinctively think, "I am getting up," or "I am going out." Is this sense of "I" mistaken? I don't believe it is. The fact that we exist as individuals is undeniable. This is affirmed by our own experience as we try to be happy and overcome difficulties, and—as Buddhists—work to attain Buddhahood for the benefit of ourselves and others. Regardless of how difficult it may be to identify just what this self is, there is something to which the thought "I am" refers: There is a "me" who "is." And it is from this "me" that our natural intuitive feelings of self arise.

It is just such a self—an atman independent of the various components that make up the personality—that the ancient Indian philosophers proposed. They subscribed to the idea of rebirth, with some adherents able to remember experiences from past lives. How else, they argued, could the continuity of an individual self over lifetimes be explained, given that the physical aspects of this self only come into being at the conception of this life? They therefore proposed a self that could continue across lifetimes while remaining independent of physical existences during individual lives.

The concept of self they put forward was singular, while the mental and physical parts we are composed of are numerous. The self was held to be permanent and unchanging, while these parts are impermanent and ever-changing. This core self was thought to be independent and autonomous, while its more exterior parts would depend on outside influences. Thus these ancient philosophers posited an atman that would be distinct from, and independent of, the mental and physical parts that make us up.

Buddha offered a radical departure from this view, proposing that the self exists merely in dependence upon its mental and physical parts. Just as there can be no bullock cart free of the parts that make it up, Buddha explained, there can be no self that exists independently of the aggregates comprising a person.

Buddha taught that to posit a unitary, unchanging, permanent, autonomous self independent of the aggregates that make up a person would introduce something that doesn't exist, and would thereby reinforce our instinctual sense of self. Buddha thus propounded the idea of selflessness—anatman.

THE EXISTENT SELF AND THE NONEXISTENT SELF

It is essential that we distinguish between the self that exists conventionally and the self that doesn't exist at all, as it is our grasping at the nonexistent self that is the source of all suffering.

Buddhist yogis—meditators—who are engaged in profound analytical meditation on the existence of self focus their analysis on their experience of "me" as an inherently real and independent self, the existence of which their meditative investigation will eventually negate. They thereby make a clear distinction between a conventional self that is the object of our reification, and the reified self that is to be negated.

In our own normal day-to-day intuitions, we have a natural and legitimate sense of self that thinks, "I'm cultivating Bodhicitta," or "I'm meditating on selflessness." A problem arises when this sense of self is too extreme, and we start to think of it as independent and autonomous—as *real*. Once we cling to such a notion, we begin to feel justified in making a stark distinction between ourselves and others. As a result of this, there is a natural tendency to regard others as totally unrelated to us, almost as objects to be exploited by this real, concrete "me." Out of this powerful attachment to a self that we falsely perceive as an identifiable, solid reality arise the equally strong attachments we develop to our belongings, our homes, our friends, and our family.

Through meditative analytical investigation we can come to recognize that at the root of the afflictions we experience lies our strong but mistaken clinging to what we perceive to be our inherently real self. From a Buddhist point of view, this sense of self is natural and also innate. In fact, Buddhists would argue that the unitary, eternal, and autonomous self postulated by non-Buddhist philosophers is a mere conceptual construct, whereas the sense of self that we innately possess is natural even in animals. If we examine the dynamic of our natural sense of self, we find that it resembles a ruler presiding over his subjects—our physical and mental parts. We have a sense that above and beyond the aggregates of body and mind, there is something we think of as "me," and that the physical and mental aggregates are dependent on "me" while "I" am autonomous. Though natural, our sense of self is mistaken, and in our quest for freedom from the miseries caused by our self-grasping, we must change our perception of ourselves.

OUR SENSE OF SELF

As long as we cling to some notion of objective existence—the idea that something actually exists in a concrete, identifiable way—emotions such as desire and aversion will follow. When we see something we like—a beautiful watch, for example—we perceive it as having some real quality of existence among its parts. We see the watch not as a collection of parts, but as an existing entity with a specific quality of watch-ness to it. And if it's a fine mechanical timepiece, our perception is enhanced by qualities that are seen to exist definitely as part of the nature of the watch. It is as a result of this misperception of the watch that our desire to possess it arises. In a similar manner, our aversion to someone we dislike arises as a result of attributing inherent negative qualities to the person.

When we relate this process to how we experience our own

sense of existence—how the thought "I" or "I am" arises—we notice that it invariably does so in relation to some aspect of our physical or mental aggregates. Our notion of ourselves is based upon a sense of our physical and emotional selves. What's more, we feel that these physical and mental aspects of ourselves exist inherently. My body is not something of which I doubt the specificity. There is a body-ness as well as a me-ness about it that very evidently exists. It seems to be a natural basis for my identifying my body as "me." Our emotions such as fear are similarly experienced as having a valid existence and as being natural bases for our identifying ourselves as "me." Both our loves and our hates serve to deepen the self sense. Even the mere feeling "I'm cold" contributes to our sense of being a solid and legitimate "I."

NEGATING THE SELF

All Buddhists advocate the cultivation of an insight into the lack—or emptiness—of self. According to Hinayana philosophers, one works to realize the absence of a self-sufficient and substantially real self. They claim that by developing one's insight into one's own personal selflessness through profound meditation over a long time—months, years, and maybe even lifetimes—one can attain liberation from the beginningless cycle of life, death, and rebirth. We shall further explore these ideas in the next chapter.

Nagarjuna, the Mahayana trailblazer who established the Middle Way school, suggests that as long as we feel that our parts or aggregates have some legitimate natural existence, we will not be able to completely eliminate our grasping at a sense of self. These aggregates are themselves composed of smaller parts and mental experiences upon which we base ourselves. He argues that in order to gain deep insight into the selflessness of person—ourselves, that is—we must develop the same insight into the selflessness of phenomena—the parts we are made up of. He states that regarding what is to be negated—the inherent existence of our own selves and the inherent existence of phenomena—it is the same. In fact, our insight into one will complement and reinforce our insight into the other.

A true understanding of emptiness of any inherent existence must touch upon the very manner in which we intuitively and instinctively perceive things. For example, when we say "this form," "this material object," we feel as if our perception of the physical object before us is true, as if there is something that the term "material object" refers to, and as if the perception that we have somehow represents what is truly there in front of us. A correct understanding of emptiness must reach that level of perception so that we no longer cling to any notion of objective inherent reality.

Nagarjuna emphasizes that so long as we impart objective reality to the world that encompasses us, we will fuel a host of thoughts and emotions such as attachment, hostility, and anger. For Nagarjuna, the understanding of selflessness arrived at by the lower Buddhist philosophical schools is not the consummation of Buddha's teaching on selflessness because there remains some trace of grasping at a notion of independent and objective, inherently existent reality. Therefore it is through cultivating insight into this most subtle meaning of emptiness—emptiness in terms of an absence of inherent existence—that one can eradicate the fundamental ignorance that binds us in samsara.

EMPTINESS OF SELF

In his work *In Praise of Dharmadhatu* (In Praise of Ultimate Expanse), Nagarjuna states:

> *Meditations on impermanence*
> *And overcoming clinging to permanence,*
> *Are all elements of training the mind.*
> *However, the supreme purification of mind*
> *Is achieved through insight into emptiness.*

Nagarjuna defines emptiness as an absence of inherent existence.

In the Heart Sutra, the Buddha makes his well-known cryptic statement,

Form is empty, emptiness is form.

There is a clearer presentation of this terse statement in the Perfection of Wisdom Sutra in 25,000 Lines, where Buddha says:

Form is not empty of emptiness;
Form itself is that emptiness.

In the first line Buddha specifies that what is being negated in respect to form is not something other than its inherent existence. In the second line he establishes the conventionally existent form that exists due to its emptiness of inherent existence. What appears when we negate the inherent existence of form, is form. The nonexistence—or emptiness—of any inherent quality of form is what enables form to exist.

Buddha pointed out that without knowledge of the emptiness of inherent existence of self there is no possibility of attaining freedom from our miserable state. The most profound meditative state of single-pointed absorption, free of all distractions of sensual experience, cannot dispel grasping at a sense of self. Sooner or later this self-grasping will serve as the basis for our experience of afflictions. These afflictions will lead to actions that will provoke more actions, resulting in our experience of misery in cyclic existence.

If, however, we had no sense of self, there would be no basis for the occurrence of attachment or aversion. Attachment comes about in response to the perception of something's being attractive. For something to be desirable there must be someone to whom it is so, as an object would not be attractive all by itself. Only when something is attractive to me do I desire it. In the same way, when something is perceived to be unattractive, aversion arises and can grow into anger and even hostility. All these strong emotions are initially due to an "I" that is experiencing a perceived attractiveness or unattractiveness of an object.

Since our experience with afflictions such as desire or aversion, pride or jealousy, is due to things being attractive or repellant to us, once the notion of this independent self is removed there is no possibility of these afflictions arising. If, however, we do not negate the mistaken notion of the "I," regardless of the profundity of our meditation, afflictions will eventually arise in us and lead to our suffering.

Buddha taught many practices by which happiness can grow

in our lives, such as acting generously toward others and rejoicing in their virtues. But as these do not directly oppose our distorted grasping at a notion of self, the qualities that these practices engender cannot provide us with the ultimate state of happiness: freedom from all suffering. Only the insight into selflessness, with its direct antidote to our ignorant self-grasping, can accomplish this.

It is essential that we penetrate the nature of phenomena by means of profound study and critical analysis. This will lead us to recognize the absence of any independent, identifiable self in all phenomena. If we then cultivate our realization of selflessness in meditation, we will eventually attain true liberation—nirvana.

THE CONTINUUM OF THE MERE I

Let us examine the elements upon which the self depends for its existence. When we identify ourselves as human beings, our identity is dependent upon our human body and our human mind. This continuum of "self," made up of a series of moments of "me," begins at birth or conception, and ends at death.

Were we not to identify ourselves as humans but merely as "me," or as the "mere I," would this self have a beginning or an end? When we look back at our past and think, "when I was young, when I became an adult," or "when I reached middle age," we personally identify with each stage, while also identifying with the continuum that spans all of the stages of our life. We are very naturally able to shift our sense of self from the present to the past, and to the totality of stages that make up a lifetime. Is it possible that this "mere I" might also extend beyond the limits of this life?

Between mind and body, it is particularly our mind or consciousness with which we identify as this "mere I." Our mind is transient, existing momentarily, each moment of consciousness affecting the next. Thus our thoughts and ideas evolve over time, as do our emotions. Change exists as well in the world of solid things. The magnificent Himalayan range may seem to have a permanent solidity, but when we view those mountains over a period of millions of years we can detect changes. In order for those changes to take place, there must be change within a time frame of one hundred years. Such change would necessitate year-by-year change, which would in turn depend upon change occurring on a monthly basis, and this would depend on smaller and smaller increments of transformation taking place from minute to minute, second to second, and at even smaller slivers of time. It is these minuscule momentary changes that form the basis for more noticeable change.

This nature of moment-by-moment change is a quality that occurs as a result of something's being produced; no other cause is necessary to bring it about.

There are certain causes that cease once their effect arises. Such causes turn into their effects, as a seed turns into a sprout. The seed is the substantial cause of the ensuing sprout. There are other causes and conditions that serve as contributory factors in bringing about an effect, such as the water, fertilizer, and sunlight that contribute to the sprouting of a seed. Taking our human body as an example, we can trace the continuum of moments leading to our present human body back to the beginning of this life, the moment of conception. This moment is called "that which is becoming human."

Our present physical body's continuum can be traced to that substantial cause—its moment of conception—which in turn can be traced back further, moment by moment, to the beginning of the universe and the subtle matter that existed at that time. From a Buddhist point of view, the continuum of substantial causes preceding our conception can be traced back to before the Big Bang, to when the universe was a void. Actually, if we follow the line of reasoning by which we trace our continuum back to before the Big Bang, we would have to acknowledge that there could not be a first moment to the continuum of substantial causes of any conditioned phenomenon.

Just as material things possess their substantial causes and their contributory conditions, mental phenomena do as well. Our feelings, our thoughts and emotions, all of which make up our consciousness, have both substantial causes that turn into a particular moment of cognition, and contributory factors that may be physical or mental.

The primary characteristic of our consciousness is its clarity and knowing. This quality of pure luminous knowing cannot be a product of a physical condition alone. From the Buddhist understanding of causality, a substantial cause must be substantially commensurate with its effect. A physical phenomenon could therefore not serve as the substantial cause of a moment of consciousness, as the nature of clarity and knowing is not physical.

Let us examine the process of conscious perception. When we see a tree, we are experiencing a mental perception of the tree before us. The tree and our physical eye serve as the contributory conditions for our conscious experience of the tree. The substantial cause of that mental experience of the tree is our immediately preceding condition of clarity and knowing. It is this preceding moment of consciousness that gives the character of clarity—of pure *knowing*—to our visual experience of the tree. Each moment of clarity and knowing in the continuum of our consciousness is caused by a preceding moment of clarity and knowing. The substantial cause of a moment of consciousness cannot be something that has a different substantial quality from clarity and knowing.

If the continuum of our mind had a first moment, it would have had to arise either from no cause or from a cause that was not substantially commensurate with the nature of mind itself. Since neither of these possibilities is acceptable, the continuum of consciousness is understood to have no beginning. This is how we explain past lives and reincarnation, given that the continuum of moments of consciousness of each of us must extend back infinite moments. And, just as the continuum of consciousness has no beginning, the identity of a self designated to that continuum is beginningless. This is corroborated by the many cases of people who recall experiences from their past lives.

And what of an end of consciousness? Some Buddhist scholars of the past maintained that upon attaining the state of nirvana the continuum of one's mental and physical existence would cease. However, an absurd consequence of this view is that there would be no one to experience the state of nirvana. The individual instances of consciousness that we experience throughout life—perceptions of all we see and feel as well as thought processes we've engaged in—will cease when our physical being expires at death. However, our fundamental quality of clarity and knowing—the essential nature of consciousness—does not end at death; its continuum is unceasing.

There also exists a very subtle physical body, referred to in Buddha's Vajrayana or Tantric teachings, that acts as the basis for our most subtle consciousness. Just as the continuum of our subtle consciousness has no beginning or end, so the continuum of this most subtle physical aspect of self is also beginningless and endless.

I find beauty in the idea of no beginning or end to the continuum of self. If there were an end to self, there would be a total annihilation, a complete darkness. For someone desperately wishing to escape the torments of life by committing suicide, such an end might seem desirable. I believe, however, that most of us prefer the idea of continuity, as it suggests a fullness of our experiences and emotions.

CHAPTER 7

The Hinayana View

THE VAIBHASHIKA, OR Great Exposition, is the first of the four Buddhist philosophical schools, and has eighteen sub-schools, some of which seem to propound a self. Vaibhashika adherents are careful, however, to claim that the self they are advocating is not eternal, unitary, or autonomous. It is by this qualification that they are held to be Buddhists.

According to Vaibhashikas, Shakyamuni Buddha spent three incalculable eons as a Bodhisattva, working toward the attainment of full enlightenment for the sake of all beings. He began his last lifetime as a Bodhisattva and attained Buddhahood while meditating under the bodhi tree in Bodh Gaya. At death Buddha's continuum of existence extinguished, like a flame upon the exhaustion of fuel.

Mahayana scholars agree with Vaibhashikas that antidotes to our mental pollutants such as attachment and aversion exist and enable us to end these pollutants. They deny, however, that there is an antidote to the actual continuum of consciousness. They therefore consider it illogical that upon a Buddha's death his consciousness itself would cease. Furthermore, it would be unreasonable for a Bodhisattva to undergo such extraordinary training over eons if this attainment were to last a mere few years.

Vaibhashikas identify the two truths—conventional and ultimate—quite differently from other schools. They define conventional truths as those phenomena that cease to be identifiable if physically or mentally broken down into parts. Ultimate truths they define as those phenomena that remain recognizable regardless of their being physically or mentally separated into parts. A glass jar would be an example of a conventional truth, because if it were to fall and break, we would no longer identify it as a glass jar. A partless particle of the sort posited by the Vaibhashikas, being by definition indivisible, would be an example of an ultimate truth. This division of the two truths differs greatly from the Madhyamika understanding that phenomena abide as conventional truths, while their emptiness of inherent existence is their ultimate nature. While to the Vaibhashikas the two truths have distinct identities, Madhyamika philosophers view the two truths as being different aspects of the same entity.

Sautrantikas, who belong to the second of the Hinayana schools, are so named because of their primary reliance on sutras, the actual teachings of the Buddha. They also divide all

phenomena into conventional and ultimate truths using a criterion different from other Buddhist schools. The guiding factor
for them is whether or not something has the ability to affect a
function. Anything able to cause a future moment of existence
is an ultimate truth. The table before me and my visual consciousness of the table are ultimate truths, as each moment of existence of the table and of my visual apprehending of the table
causes its next moment of existence. Phenomena that abide in our
minds—objects of thought such as the mental image of a table
when I think of a table—are not able to perform functions and
do not exist momentarily; they are therefore conventional truths.

While all other schools contend that a cause must naturally
precede its effect, Vaibhashikas contend that there are certain
causes that exist simultaneously with their effects. An example
would be consciousness apprehending a flower through the eye
and the simultaneous feeling of pleasure accompanying that
sight. Sautrantikas, along with the Mahayana Buddhist schools,
reject that the mind that sees the flower could be the cause of
its concurrent feeling of pleasure, as the experience of pleasure
would necessarily follow the initial perception of the flower.

Vaibhashikas maintain that when sense perceptions arise,
there is no mediating aspect; there is a naked mirroring of the
object. Sautrantikas, along with the other Buddhist schools,

contend that when sense perceptions arise, a mediating likeness or aspect is experienced. This seems to resemble current scientific understanding.

This is but a brief overview of the two Hinayana schools of philosophy. I hope that readers will explore these further, as our understanding of the lower rungs of our ladder will greatly benefit our understanding of the subtler philosophical tenets found in the Mahayan schools of the higher rungs.

CHAPTER 8

THE MIND-ONLY VIEW

CITTAMATRA, OR MIND-ONLY, is the first of the Great Vehicle or Mahayana schools. Its name reflects the view that phenomena are of one entity with the mind that perceives them. When we see a table, the table that we perceive is said to be of the same nature as our mind perceiving it.

How does this work in practice? The tables and chairs, smells and sounds that I experience are said by Mind-Only philosophers to come into being as a result of my past actions, my karma, which causes the predisposition or potential to experience these things. My virtuous past karma instigates pleasant experiences, sweet smells, and lovely sounds, while my non-virtue brings about the unpleasant. If you and I happen to share the pleasure of a sweet-smelling flower, this shared experience arises from our each having the predisposition to experience the lovely sight and sweet smell of the flower as a result of our own individual past actions or karma; but the flowers that we each experience, though seemingly one, are held to be distinct, as they are the manifestations of our own distinct karmas.

Since Mind-Only philosophers agree that a cause must precede its effect, they contend that the flower does not act as a cause for the eye consciousness experiencing it, as other Buddhist schools would hold. Instead, being the same entity as its apprehending consciousness, the flower exists simultaneously with that consciousness.

This Mind-Only understanding of how a flower exists does not diminish the solidity of the flower. Their position is that although the flower doesn't exist independently of my experience of it, it must exist truly and inherently in order to exist at all.

According to the Mind-Only view, things do not exist independently of our mental experience of them. Given that things manifest as a result of our deserving to experience them, they have no basis for existing free of our experience of them. In our ignorance, however, we wrongly perceive things to exist independently of our perceptions, as if they had their own independent lives. As this perception of separateness of subject and object is held by Cittamatra philosophers to be faulty, the aim of a Mind-Only practitioner or yogi is to remove it.

Buddha taught that phenomena may be divided into three natures. These are the other-powered, the imputed, and the thoroughly established. Mind-Only philosophers explain other-powered natures to be impermanent things such as tables and chairs. Their existence independent of a consciousness apprehending them is held to be their imputed nature, while their lack of such an independent existence is their thoroughly established nature. According to Mind-Only philosophers, the imputed nature of our tables and chairs doesn't actually exist. Recognition of this nonexistence is what Mind-Only yogis pursue in their meditation.

Another aspect of the thoroughly established nature of things is that names and labels do not naturally refer to them. Tables and chairs seem to be the natural bases for being called tables and chairs. They seem to possess this quality by way of their own character, independently of our naming them. Mind-Only philosophers point out that if this were so, then the name "table" would apply to the table before it was ever named "table," and that nothing else could possibly be called "table."

If we look at a bottle, we feel that it possesses the innate criterion for being called "bottle." We do not feel that the name "bottle" is merely a label that is conveniently given to the object. We feel as if there is some natural relationship between the bottle and its name, "bottle," and that the bottle came into being possessing the quality of being the natural referent of the term "bottle." If this were the case, Mind-Only philosophers argue, how could one particular object—our bottle for example—ever possess more than its one natural name? And how could many objects possess the same name?

The realization that phenomena are not the natural referents of names is said to be equal to realizing the lack of separateness between objects and the minds perceiving them.

It should be noted that there are existent imputed natures such as permanent phenomena, which would include the concept of space, and there are nonexistent ones such as the child of a barren woman. These are not, however, of interest to yogis who are trying to free themselves from their natural inclination to view themselves and the rest of phenomena as independent of their mental experience of them.

CHAPTER 9

THE MIDDLE WAY

THE MIDDLE WAY referred to in the name of this philosophical school is a position that avoids the two extremes of nihilism and absolutism. Nihilism is a denial of the existence of all reality, even conventional existence. Absolutism is a belief in any true, substantial, or independent existence. Rejection of these two extremes assumes a position that holds all that exists to be dependently originated.

Things are understood to depend upon their causes in the way a clay pot depends on the clay of which it is formed. Similarly, phenomena depend upon their constituents as an orange depends on its sections and peel, and as the great expanse of space depends on the space in each direction.

Nagarjuna and his Madhyamika followers reject the notion of any substantial reality or true existence of things and events. They deny that things exist independently of our apprehending them. A chair, they hold, does not exist as a chair in any manner beyond its being identified as a chair.

Some of Nagarjuna's interpreters hold that though phenomena may ultimately be empty of inherent existence, on the conventional level they must exist inherently. These Middle Way Autonomists are named for the type of logical sign they consider essential to a yogi generating an initial realization of emptiness. They contend that for a chair to be established as a chair, it must exist as such from its own side: it must possess some inherent quality of chair-ness. Middle Way Autonomists also accept that, on the whole, our sensory perceptions are not mistaken with respect to the objects they experience, since to them the appearance of chair-ness—that independently established quality of the chair—is not incorrect.

Another group of Madhyamika thinkers are the Middle Way Consequentialists, so labeled for their assertion that a logical consequence is sufficient for a yogi to realize emptiness. They reject any notion of inherent reality, even on the conventional level. The chair, they say, possesses no inherent existence—no quality of chair-ness—even though such a quality appears to exist. Hence, the Middle Way Consequentialists maintain that there is not a single instance of our conventional awareness that is not mistaken or distorted by the appearance of inherent reality. It is only the mental state of meditative equipoise of a yogi realizing emptiness directly that is undistorted, as in such a state all that appears to the yogi is the emptiness or lack of inherent existence.

All followers of Nagarjuna agree that in our normal way of seeing a chair, it seems to exist inherently; a quality of chair-ness appears to us. We clearly identify the object before us as a chair. What Nagarjuna's followers argue over is whether or not this chair-ness does indeed exist from the side of the object, established by way of its own character. In other words, whether there is indeed a chair to be found if we were to search among the parts of that which we've identified as a chair before us. The Autonomists claim that if the chair didn't exist inherently there would be no chair at all. Thus, to them, the appearance of chair-ness, or some inherent quality of the chair, would not be a mistaken perception of the chair. It would actually be an essential quality for a chair to exist. The Consequentialists counter that nothing could possibly exist inherently, and therefore any appearance of inherent existence would be mistaken.

Some Middle Way Autonomists explain the way things conventionally exist in a manner similar to Mind-Only philosophers. They claim that the various things we interact with—tables and chairs, friends and foes—are of the same essence as the consciousness apprehending them. Thus the table and our mind perceiving it are of the same essence or nature. These Middle

Way Autonomists differ, however, with the Mind-Only view on whether or not the table does truly and substantially exist. To the Autonomists, if the table is of the same nature as the mind apprehending it, then it doesn't exist truly or substantially, while Mind-Only philosophers claim that if the table didn't exist substantially it couldn't exist at all. Other Autonomists contend that things exist just as they appear to, separate from—though not fully independently of—the mind apprehending them.

All followers of Nagarjuna's Middle Way agree that ultimately—that is, for an ultimate consciousness experiencing the ultimate truth—things are empty of any quality of existence at all, since emptiness of inherent existence is all that will be experienced by that ultimate consciousness. Emptiness is the ultimate truth. It is what a yogi apprehends when focused on the ultimate.

To experience this ultimate truth we must go beyond our conventional way of perceiving the chair before us and analyze it by searching for the existence of a chair that would be independent of our perception of it. In our investigation we mentally sift through all the parts that make up the chair—the four legs, the seat, the back—in search of a chair that stands alone, independent of those parts. We come to the conclusion that there is nothing there that can be identified as a chair free of our mentally labeling the assembled parts a chair.

A meditator who has searched for an independently existent chair among the parts will then direct his or her mind single-pointedly at the non-findability of such a chair. By concentrating to the point where the meditator clearly experiences that non-findability of such a chair, he or she will be experiencing a realization of the emptiness of a truly existent chair.

Such an experience is initially brought about by a process of logical reasoning, resulting in an inference of the emptiness of a truly existent chair. This inferential experience of emptiness appears to the yogi conceptually. If, however, the yogi remains concentrated on the inferred emptiness, he or she will eventually experience that emptiness of a truly existent chair directly, seeing it as clearly as I do the lines on the palm of my hand. At this point it is said that the mind experiencing emptiness and the emptiness being perceived are of one taste, similar to water being poured into water. There is no longer a duality of subject and object. The yogi has attained a stage of meditation called the Path of Seeing, and is referred to as a Noble One.

Nagarjuna's interpreters agree that the ultimate level of consciousness—this mental state of meditative equipoise—directly realizes the emptiness of any true, substantial quality of the chair. The difference of opinion among Nagarjuna's main followers regards whether the chair does in fact exist inherently. To the Autonomists the chair would have to, as otherwise it could not exist at all. How could a chair exist without having some chair-ness to it? The idea would seem absurd: a chairless chair? The Consequentialists respond that if the chair did indeed exist inherently, then that intrinsic quality of the chair should be identifiable and would necessarily reveal itself to the investigative consciousness of a Noble One who is single-pointedly focused on searching for it. This investigative consciousness of such a yogi actually discovers that chair-ness to be lacking! How, they retort, can one hold something to exist if its nonexistence is directly experienced at the most profound level? These latter interpreters, therefore, assert that all of our common perceptions of phenomena are necessarily mistaken, given that things always appear to exist inherently.

Though it might be thought that the emptiness that is experienced by the meditator would possess some quality of objective existence, this emptiness is merely the *non-findability* of any quality of inherent existence of the chair. Emptiness itself lacks any findable reality; it too would reveal itself to be empty of inherent existence if it were the focus of the yogi's investigation. Hence we distinguish between what is witnessed from such an ultimate perspective and what can withstand ultimate analysis. Emptiness is what is witnessed, but *nothing* can withstand ultimate analysis, not even the emptiness that is witnessed from the ultimate perspective.

How Do Things Exist?

If things don't exist the way we perceive them to—possessing an objective identifiable reality—then how are we to understand their existence? How can things be? How can they function? If we are claiming that a chair does not inherently exist, then how do we explain a chair's ability to perform the function it does, enabling us to sit on it?

All Buddhists accept the existence of things. No one is denying that our chair is there to sit on. The Middle Way Autonomists, accepting that things do exist inherently, hold that all names and labels must refer to things that are substantially real. When we refer to something that we call a "rose," there must be something that we can identify and point to that is actually a rose. Similarly, a person is imputed upon the combination of a physical human body and a mind. Autonomists claim that the true referent of the label "person" must be found among the parts that make the person up. In this regard, some Middle Way Autonomists propose the mental continuum of the individual to be the true referent of the term "person," while others suggest a separate consciousness they call the mind-basis-of-all.

The Middle Way Consequentialists, rejecting any notion of inherent existence, argue that just as there is no chair to be found among its parts and no rose to be found among its petals, so there is no person to be found among its constituent aspects of body and mind. Moreover, each part of the person, subjected to the same scrutiny, will reveal itself to be equally unfindable among the parts that make it up. My arm, made up of bones, flesh, muscle, skin, and so forth, cannot be identified among its parts. "Arm" is merely a name imputed in dependence upon the parts. My mental continuum, made up of a series of moments of consciousness, is also merely a label imputed in dependence upon all of those moments of consciousness. Each of the physical and mental parts of which I am composed is similarly empty of any identifiable existence. Consequentialists thus conclude that nothing can exist inherently, whether conventionally or ultimately.

Our initial reaction to recognizing that things do not possess objective or inherent existence is understandably one of surprise. We are discovering that the actual way things exist is so very contrary to how we naturally relate to them. However, as we deepen our understanding and accustom ourselves to a correct view of the world, we will eventually come to feel, "Of course, things cannot possess inherent existence. This *must* be the way things exist." If things did possess some inherent quality of existence, then such an independent characteristic would necessarily be born out by our search for it. Instead, investigation clearly reveals a lack of any such existence.

Nagarjuna suggests in *The Precious Garland* that just as a mirage appears from a distance to be water, while up close revealing itself not to be, the mind and body seem to be the self, while when examined closely, prove not to be.

If we do not know why the Buddha taught about emptiness, we will misunderstand emptiness itself. We need to recognize that our clinging to the inherent existence of things is the basis for afflictions such as attachment and aversion and all ensuing misery. Conversely, by countering our natural grasping at inherent existence we remove the basis for suffering.

As Shantideva reminds us in his *Guide to the Bodhisattva's Way of Life*, it is not the objects of the world around us that are being refuted by the concept of emptiness, it is our perception that those objects possess a true, inherent existence that we work to reverse, because this grasping is the cause of all our misery.

The quality of existence that must be negated in order to altogether uproot the cause of our suffering is of the subtlest nature. The refutation of a unitary, unchanging, and independent self will not suffice, nor will the denial of a self-sufficient and substantially existent self. If we do not counter a quality of inherent existence, then the basis for our grasping at self will remain.

Nagarjuna tells us, "The key characteristic of emptiness is its ability to dissolve all conceptual elaborations." It is therefore essential that we negate any vestige of objective reality in order to undo the workings of our fundamental ignorance and thereby remove the possibility of afflictions and their ensuing misery.

It is important to note that the negation of this nonexistent quality does not imply the existence of anything in its stead. It is a mere nonaffirming negation, comparable to my stating that there is no television in my room. In no way do I suggest that there is anything else in the room. Similarly, emptiness of inherent existence does not imply the existence of any other quality. Emptiness refers just to the nonexistence of inherent existence.

THE AFFLICTIONS

If we examine our psychological processes, especially when we experience strong emotions such as attachment or anger, our grasping at the objective reality of things gives rise to a distorted way of perceiving the world. When we find something attractive, then we superimpose upon that object qualities of desirability that are over and above what is justified. Our feeling of attachment toward the object then grows into desire. Similarly, when we find something unattractive, we instantly superimpose on it an exaggerated quality of undesirability. This then gives rise to a reaction of repulsion or aversion toward the object, which culminates in feelings such as anger, hostility, or hatred. Underlying our complex afflictive emotions is our distorted way of perceiving the quality of objects, which stems from a deeply embedded belief that things and events possess some form of objective and inherent reality. This is why it is crucial that we correct our distorted way of viewing the world.

How do we go about removing this fundamental delusion? We can't do so simply by making a wish, "May my grasping at inherent existence disappear." Nor can we do so by means of a blessing from someone. Our fundamentally distorted way of perceiving ourselves and the world around us can only be altered by our cultivating a valid perception that opposes the faulty way we naturally perceive things. This valid perception is a true insight into emptiness.

It is helpful to understand what I would call the law of opposite forces. We are familiar with the law of opposite forces operating in the material world. If we find a room too cold, we can turn up the heat. If we find it too hot, we turn it down. The law of opposite forces works here because heat and cold do not reside simultaneously without one undermining the other. Similarly, we can remove darkness in a room by switching on the light.

Just as the law of opposite forces operates in a variety of ways within the natural world, it also operates in our mental world. In order to counter our negative emotions such as anger and hatred, we cultivate loving-kindness and compassion. Similarly, to counter strong feelings of lust and attachment we meditate on the impurity and impermanence of the object of our desire. Our thought process opposes our afflictive emotions and gradually diminishes them.

Such antidotes will only undermine our afflictions; they will not eliminate them totally. A realization of emptiness, because it is grounded in insight, has a radical effect upon our negative mental tendencies, similar to switching on a light in a dark room, as it immediately dispels our habitual ignorant grasping at inherent existence.

Some of our afflictions have a cognitive character, while others are more impulsive in nature. Anger and attachment, for example, are impulsive, possessing a far lower cognitive character. Our fundamental ignorance has a much higher cognitive quality. Therefore, in order to counter it we must cultivate its direct opposite, the wisdom realizing emptiness.

Although both wisdom and ignorance are mental qualities, the power of our fundamental ignorance comes primarily from long habituation. However, our fundamental ignorance is at odds with the way things actually are: There is, in reality, no basis for our mistaken perception, and no valid support for it in reason. In contrast, though emptiness may initially be difficult to understand, the concept of emptiness is in accord with reality, as it is grounded in valid experience and can withstand logical scrutiny.

Once we have cultivated wisdom realizing emptiness, we must increase its potential by developing familiarity with it. Our wisdom will thereby gradually reach a point where it can eradicate our fundamental ignorance.

Furthermore, the essential nature of our mind is its clarity and luminosity. These qualities of mind are pure and unpolluted. Through our prolonged cultivation of wisdom, it is possible to eradicate our fundamental ignorance to the point where the afflictions, along with any propensity toward afflictive thought arising in dependence upon our ignorance, are eliminated. This possibility of removing all obstacles to pure luminosity and knowing suggests our potential to attain a state of omniscience.

DEPENDENT ORIGINATION

So, who am I? Who or what is at the core of me? Am I any of the individual mental or physical elements that make up what I think of as "me"? Or am I a mere combination of them? If I am not identifiable with the individual elements of the body, and yet cannot be identified with the collection of these elements, then who am I? Could I be identified as something separate from and independent of these physical elements? This possibility is also untenable; how could I be independent of the parts that make me up?

Nagarjuna demonstrates that the concept of "me" is to be understood as merely a label that is designated in dependence upon the collection of parts—physical and mental—that make me up. If something is designated, it evidently doesn't exist independently, as that designation depends upon the basis it is designated to. If something possesses a dependent nature, then it cannot exist independently as dependence and independence are mutually exclusive. Hence the concept of "me" is not independently or inherently existent, given that something's being dependently existent contradicts its existing independently.

The true meaning of emptiness must be understood in terms of dependent origination. As Nagarjuna says in the same text, "That which is dependently originated has been taught to be empty, and that I call the Middle Way." The dependence he refers to cannot be limited to causal dependence in the sense that a sprout is contingent on a seed, or that our suffering ensues from our previous nonvirtuous actions. In order to refute inherent existence, our comprehension of dependent origination must recognize dependent designation. It is only when we understand the chair to exist merely in dependence upon our identifying it as such that we are getting at a notion of dependent origination that can undermine our natural view of the chair as existing inherently.

Similarly, in viewing ourselves we must recognize that "I" exist merely in dependence upon designating a quality of self to the mental and physical parts that are the basis for my identification of "me."

Emptiness is a quality of all phenomena. As Nagarjuna states, "There is no phenomenon that is not dependently originated; there is nothing that is not empty."

Once we understand emptiness in the sense of dependent origination—and dependent designation in particular—we will know that things exist by mere designation and labeling. A table is designated or labeled a table in dependence upon its base of designation: the parts of a table. Those parts are not the table; they are the basis upon which we identify something as "table." There is no inherently existent table among its parts. If we search among those parts—the tabletop, its sides and legs—we will not turn up an identifiable table hidden among those parts. Also, the idea of our table turning up separately from those parts is absurd. How could a table exist devoid of any parts?

It is important to clarify that our table, which exists by mere designation or labeling, and the name "table," are not one and the same thing. The name "table" is a word and therefore part of language, while the table is a piece of furniture upon which we place things.

As I've said above, this unfindability of our table is a quality that applies to all other things as well. We can look for the car among its parts, the house among its parts, and the tree among the root, trunk, branches, and leaves, and we will find no car, no house, and no tree. The same is true of sounds and smells, each of which has parts that form the basis for our identifying them as sounds or smells. Similarly, everything within the realm of existence, whether produced or conceptualized, exists by mere imputation. This status of phenomena is their emptiness. This is not emptiness in the sense of an empty room; it is an emptiness of any findable quality of room-ness among the parts that make up the room.

ALL PHENOMENA ARISE FROM EMPTINESS

As Nagarjuna states in his *Commentary on the Awakening Mind*, "If we understand all phenomena to be empty, the relationship of cause and effect—karma and its fruits—becomes tenable. This is indeed a great wonder, more wondrous than the most wonderful, more amazing than the most amazing!"

By understanding emptiness in terms of dependent origination, we can establish the functionality of things. We can recognize the relationship between causes and their effects to be interdependent and thefore necessarily independent of each other. If something were to possess an inherent, objective existence, it would become a self-enclosed reality that would prohibit it from interrelating with other phenomena. Hence it is this lack of inherent existence—this emptiness—that enables a thing to function, to be produced, to produce, and to interact with other things.

DEPENDENT DESIGNATION

As I have said earlier, the principle of dependent origination—pratityasamutpada—is a defining characteristic of Buddhist philosophy. There are different levels of understanding of pratityasamutpada, beginning with the dependence of things and events on their causes and conditions. All Buddhists accept this level, which only applies to conditioned things. Next is the understanding of dependent origination in respect to the relationship between parts and a whole. Ultimately we come to the concept of dependent designation that we have been discussing.

The first of these three dependent relationships is limited to effects resulting from their causes. The relationship is valid in only one temporal direction, as the flow of time from past to future prohibits a cause from depending on its effect in the sense of resulting from it.

Considered more subtly, we recognize that just as something can only be identified as an effect in respect to its cause, the reverse is also true: A cause can only be identified as a cause in respect to its effect. How could something be a cause if it were not the cause of an effect? Its causal identity is therefore dependent on its subsequent effect. In this sense, the dependent relationship operates in both temporal directions.

Though a cause cannot be the effect of itself, nevertheless it is necessarily the effect of a cause other than itself. The sprout is the effect of its causal seed while also being the cause of the future tree. This demonstrates that no cause is an absolute cause, in and of itself. Causes are only causes in dependence upon their effects, while also being effects in dependence upon their own causes. Anything may therefore be called a cause in dependence upon its having an effect, and an effect in dependence upon its having been caused. Nothing has the slightest inherent quality of being either a cause or an effect, as this would prohibit the cause being anything but a cause, or the effect being anything but an effect.

Taking the example of a wooden chair, we can understand that the tree of which it is made is a cause of the chair. The existence of the chair depends on that tree; there would be no chair without the tree. The tree, however, cannot be said to depend on the chair in any causal sense. Similarly, in a temporal manner we can say that the chair of today is the effect of the chair of yesterday, each moment of our chair being the cause of the next moment of the chair. Here again, the existence of the chair today—the resultant chair—depends upon the existence of the chair yesterday—the causal chair. It is more difficult to say that the chair of yesterday depends upon the chair of today. We can recognize, however, that the causal chair can only be considered a causal chair in relation to a resultant chair, as cause without an effect would be meaningless.

Let us take this one step farther. Though today's chair results from the chair of yesterday, it also causes the chair of tomorrow. Hence today's chair is not inherently a resultant chair. It is only dependently so, designated so in dependence upon its being the effect of the causal chair of the day before. Just as it needs the chair of yesterday to be a resultant chair, so it needs the chair of tomorrow to be a causal chair.

A coarser understanding of dependent origination will prepare one to grasp its subtler interpretations. Conversely, our understanding of emptiness as mere designation enables us to better understand the dependent relationship between things and their parts, which will in turn deepen our understanding of the mechanics of cause and effect.

As we develop our insight into emptiness, we must also work to purify our motives for pursuing this wisdom aspect of the path to enlightenment. Wisdom alone will not lead us to the ultimate state of Buddhahood. We must develop the method aspect of the path by which we can serve our fellow sentient beings and lead them toward happiness and freedom from all levels of suffering.

CHAPTER 10

The Method Aspect of the Path

AS SPIRITUAL PRACTITIONERS we strive for simplicity. Avoiding excessive attention to our own comfort, we also avoid an overly ascetic lifestyle, since true spiritual practice aims at transforming our mental state, not at mastering physical penance. We should be clear that this is not some dictate to be followed because Buddha told us to avoid excesses. It is we who suffer as a result of indulgence or asceticism. By diminishing our tendency toward these extremes, we bring more happiness to our own lives.

It is best, I believe, for a lay practitioner to remain involved in society while leading a spiritual life. Though some exceptional individuals may be capable of dedicating themselves totally to profound meditative practices, I myself try to follow a middle path, balancing spiritual concerns with worldly responsibility.

Mind Training

The essence of mind training is the cultivation of Bodhicitta, the altruistic mind seeking to attain the full enlightenment of a Buddha in order to most effectively benefit all sentient beings. We begin our training by reflecting on the disadvantages of self-cherishing and the advantages of working for the well-being of others. This we do by means of analytical meditation, calmly scrutinizing and contemplating these notions over many months and even years, so that we may eventually perceive others to be more important than we ourselves.

In this practice we also learn to turn our adversities into opportunities. We must not expect that the challenging situations we encounter in life will change, but by altering our attitude toward these situations, we are able to view difficulty not as something we wish to hide from, but as an opportunity to work on ourselves. This will naturally help us to withstand situations we might previously have thought unbearable. Thus, for an advanced mind-training practitioner, even conditions that would normally seem to be obstacles to spiritual growth, such as illness leading to a shortened life, can become opportunities for inner development. One past practitioner has said, "I will be unhappy when things are prosperous and will rejoice when they are not, as that is when spiritual practice occurs."

For most of us, our image of ourselves as spiritual practitioners is dependent upon things going well for us. The great

Tibetan master Togmey Zangpo wrote, "When the sun is shining and the belly is full there is the form of holiness, however when faced with adversity, no trace can be found of the truly holy one." When things are going well we see ourselves as practitioners, but when challenges arise, any trace of virtue seems to vanish. We will argue with our fellow beings, even insulting them when necessary.

A true spiritual practitioner, particularly one engaged in mind training, is able to use misfortune for spiritual practice. The practitioner would rather be disparaged than praised. When we are admired there is danger of pride arising, causing arrogance toward inferiors, jealousy toward superiors, and competition toward rivals. We are less likely to experience these emotions without an inflated sense of self.

If we enjoy success in life, we should avoid conceit and, instead, use the opportunity to appreciate the results of virtue and determine to practice it as often as possible. If we wish to be true practitioners of mind training then we must skillfully transform any conceivable event to enhance our commitment to others. When even an inkling of arrogance arises within us, the thought of Bodhicitta should deflate it. And when faced with tragedy, instead of feeling demoralized, we should utilize the situation to further enhance our practice by considering the countless beings suffering in similar and even greater ways. Shantideva, in his *Guide to the Bodhisattva's Way of Life*, expresses this sentiment in a verse I find particularly inspiring:

> *For as long as space remains,*
> *As long as sentient beings remain,*
> *May I too remain*
> *To dispel their misery.*

Thus, training our mind enhances Bodhicitta in a most skillful way, molding our mental faculties and enabling us to appreciate and benefit from the difficulties that would otherwise cause us misery.

HOW TO ORDER OUR PRACTICE

It is important that we order our practices correctly. We begin by reflecting on the rarity and preciousness of our human life. We then contemplate our impermanence and our inevitable death. We consider the laws of karma—cause and effect—and how pain results from our nonvirtuous actions while happiness stems from virtue. Finally, we contemplate the suffering that pervades our lives within the cycle of life and death. These preliminary thoughts enable us to develop compassion toward the infinite sentient beings who, like us, suffer within samsara. Compassion—the wish to free them from suffering—will lead us to recognize the need to develop our ability to help them and will serve as the seed of Bodhicitta.

Whether or not we are able to generate Bodhicitta is determined by the power of our compassion. Crucial to cultivating compassion is our feeling of closeness to others and our understanding of the nature of the suffering we wish them to be free of. The more clearly we see the plight of others, the more our hearts will go out to them.

Initially, it is easier to recognize our own dissatisfied state of being. We must identify and acknowledge it to the point of revulsion. This will lead us to feel disgust for our afflictive mental attitudes and habits, the conditions that have caused our situation. We need to contemplate the destructive nature of these afflictions, as they are the origins of our misery. For this we must understand the mechanics of karma.

Karma, as we have discussed earlier, refers to the dynamic by which certain actions give rise to certain consequences. This must be recognized, understood, and pondered in meditation so that we may acknowledge that it is our own actions—particularly our mental actions—that are responsible for our difficulties in life.

We must also bring a sense of urgency to our practice by reflecting on death and impermanence. A mere acknowledgment that we will eventually die is not enough. We must recognize the danger that we may die without having seized the opportunity accorded us by our human existence. This is not a fear of death, but rather a concern that we may die without utilizing this wonderful human life. For this recognition we need to truly appreciate the preciousness of the human existence we possess.

We therefore begin our meditation by contemplating the value of our human life and the opportunities it offers. We intensify our determination to make good use of this life by pondering our imminent death. We proceed by considering the workings of karma, and the miserable nature of cyclic existence. This thought process naturally leads to a renunciation of any involvement with the affairs of samsara.

To gain true appreciation for this human birth, a mind-training practitioner meditates on the other life forms in existence. Buddhism propounds three lower realms that one may be born into as a result of selfishly motivated actions committed at the expense of others. Powerful negative behavior causes the intense suffering experienced in either hot or cold hells, while less powerful acts bring about the pain of hunger experienced by *pretas*—hungry ghosts—who are unable to satisfy their appetite. Mild negativity propels one into a lifetime as an animal whose ignorance inhibits its spiritual development and whose base ways cause it more suffering. In addition to the human realm that we have the extraordinary fortune to share, there are the god and demigod realms into which one is born as a result of neutral or virtuous acts.

This is a simplified description of our Buddhist view of the different realms of existence. It is for each of us to research and consider the workings of karma so that we become inspired to behave in ways that lead to happiness for ourselves and for those around us.

When we've contemplated the intense suffering experienced in lower realms and developed appreciation for our human condition, we recognize that death will very likely prevent us from completing our life's work. Our fear of not making use of this human opportunity will lead us to reflect on how our own selfishly motivated actions cause our suffering and how our virtuous behavior results in happiness.

From this reflection will grow understanding of how our afflictions imprison us in a perpetual state of misery within cyclic existence, which in turn will increase our desire to extract ourselves from samsara. Our renunciation of any involvement in the affairs of cyclic existence is a major spiritual step, not to be seen as the purging of friends, family, and physical belongings, but rather as a shift in our attitude toward these. We are no longer devoting ourselves to worldly concerns, but are instead working toward our attainment of freedom from the fetters of such concerns, and particularly from the afflictions such as desire and anger that bind us in samsara.

The greater our sense of revulsion toward our afflictions, and the more penetrating our insight into the nature of our own suffering, the more profound will be our compassion when we shift our attention to others. We acknowledge that just as we wish not to suffer, others wish the same. When we see them caught in the vicious circle of their misery, our sense of compassion will grow, as will our aversion to the afflictive attitudes that cause their suffering. As a result, our recognition of our powerlessness will inspire us to attain the ultimate state of enlightenment. This is the aspiration of Bodhicitta.

SUFFERING

As I have stated earlier, when we contemplate the suffering of all sentient beings, it is particularly the all-pervasive nature of this suffering of conditioning that we should focus on. What is the nature of this pervasive suffering? It is our very situation under the control of habits resulting from our past actions and afflictions. It is therefore essential that we cultivate a wish that all sentient beings overcome this most subtle conditioned suffering that pervades their existence for as long as they remain in cyclic existence.

It is important that we understand just how truly all-pervasive suffering is. We naturally feel sympathy for an elderly beggar on the street. We are less likely to feel compassion for a successful person enjoying his wealth and power—we are more likely to feel envy!—but this would indicate our failure to appreciate the fact that all conditioned existence is characterized by pain. Though our beggar's situation is surely unfortunate, his modest concerns, limited as they are to finding food and a place to sleep, might enable him to have a far more peaceful mind, free of the expectation, competition, anticipation, and frustrations of our successful person. When we realize how enslaved he or she is by strong destructive emotions, we can begin to understand that the successful person is just as deserving of compassion. By expanding such lines of contemplation we can extend our compassion to include even those who harm us.

MECHANICS OF KARMA

From a Buddhist perspective, if the victim of a harmful act isn't behaving under the influence of destructive emotions, he or she won't accrue the negativity that would otherwise cause him or her more harm in the future. Also, but through enduring harmful acts with an attitude of acceptance, an individual can exhaust the force of the past negativity he or she committed—negativity that, from the perspective of karma, is considered to be the actual cause of the harm he or she is presently facing. In other words, if someone hits me, I am experiencing the consequence of some non-virtue I committed in the past. By being hit I exhaust the potential of that particular past nonvirtue to cause me harm.

Anger and desire frequently go together. When we experience a strong desire for a seemingly unattainable object, and perceive someone to be inhibiting the fulfillment of our desire, we will get angry. Underlying that anger will be a strong attachment to the desired object. We will become consumed by a sense of "self" desiring the object. We will grasp simultaneously at the intrinsic reality we falsely impute to the desired object, and at the equally false sense of self at the core of our desiring. At this point we are under the influence of all three of the root afflictions—attachment, anger, and ignorance—and if we allow this, we will be the victim of still more suffering.

Of course, it is difficult to keep all this in mind when we are actually suffering misfortune. As a result, we must seek to contemplate these facts when in calm circumstances. Through focused analytical meditation, we can gradually habituate our minds to this new attitude toward perceived injustices and misfortunes. Over time this new attitude will provide us more tolerance, enabling us to remain more patient when we find ourselves unjustly provoked. It may take years of practice before we notice any change in ourselves, but perseverance will *definitely* bear fruit.

How to Think About the Three Jewels

We have discussed the importance of recognizing the preciousness and impermanence of our human existence, of understanding the laws of cause and effect or karma, and of contemplating the all-pervasive nature of suffering. In addition, we should learn to appreciate the refuge that the Buddhist path offers from these conditions. We must appreciate what is meant by Dharma as true cessation, for this is the essential object of all our work as Buddhist practitioners. Without this possibility of bringing the chain of karma to a halt, there is little point in thinking about the rarity and preciousness of our human existence, as we would not recognize the opportunity it accords us. We must understand that freedom from our miserable samsaric situation is possible, and that we have the ability to bring about this freedom. We will thereby come to truly appreciate the opportunity our human life grants us.

Contemplating our impermanence and imminent death will give more of a sense of urgency to our use of our current human incarnation. Without an appreciation for the opportunities our fleeting human life accords us, I feel that our contemplation of death would seem depressing and even masochistic.

With our practice ordered in this way, we will appreciate the value of a spiritual guide or teacher, as we will recognize that a true master can provide the possibility for liberation from the vicious circle of samsara. I am not speaking here of any teacher, but of a qualified master who has deep faith in the Buddha, the Dharma, and the Sangha—the Three Jewels in which we as Buddhists take refuge. Such a teacher must possess the motivation or intention to live his or her life in accordance with Buddha's teachings. When these qualities are present in a teacher, he or she becomes an embodiment of the Dharma.

It is in our analytical meditation that we subject the Dharma to critical scrutiny and thereby strengthen our admiration and faith in the Buddha as a truly authentic teacher of his doctrine the Dharma. This will enhance our understanding of the Buddhist path, and our admiration for the Sangha—those who are engaged with us in walking the path—will also increase.

GIVING AND TAKING

We should work toward cherishing the welfare of others to the point where we are unable to bear the sight of their misery. As we cannot actually remove their suffering, we work on ourselves by means of a practice called *giving and taking*. We imagine giving all our positive qualities, our prosperity, our resources and possessions, to others, and taking upon ourselves all their difficulties. In our meditation we attempt to feel the suffering of others as so unbearable that our feelings of compassion toward them will reach a kind of boiling point.

We engage in the meditative practice of giving and taking—*tonglen* as it is called in Tibetan—with deeply felt compassion that wishes to assume all suffering, from the pain of a specific illness to the more generalized suffering of conditioned existence. We begin by imagining that we are taking upon ourselves all others' misery. We then offer all of our prosperity, happiness, and virtues to them. This imaginary taking reinforces our compassion for all sentient beings, while giving strengthens our love for them.

Though there are some who can immediately practice taking on the suffering of others, for most it is easier to begin by taking on our own future suffering. We envision ourselves destitute and desperate, with no recourse and no protection. We visualize actually taking this situation upon ourselves. This will help us to better comprehend and assume the true suffering of others.

We can eventually correlate this practice with breathing, imagining that as we inhale we are taking upon ourselves all the suffering of others, and as we exhale we are providing them with our prosperity and happiness.

As mind-training practitioners, we work to incorporate all situations of life into our practice. When we come across things we desire or dislike, we must train our minds to immediately recognize our feelings of desire or repulsion and seize the opportunity to transform them constructively. We ask, "May this experience of desire save others from experiencing the same, and may they thereby avoid the repercussions of selfish attitudes." When faced with an unwanted situation, a disliked object, or a hostile provocation, as we sense anger arising we must have the presence of mind to think, "May my experience of anger serve to free all others harmed by similar afflictive emotions."

It is helpful to recite inspiring words such as these from *The Precious Garland* of Nagarjuna: "May all the suffering and problems of others ripen upon me, and may all my virtue, prosperity, and happiness blossom upon them." Repeating such words helps us to internalize them.

GENERATING BODHICITTA

We must keep in mind that our practice works—that it can result in the decrease of our own suffering and that of others. When the discerning Buddhist practitioner extends his or her concern to include all others, the knowledge that their misery really and truly can be eliminated will naturally intensify the wish for this to happen. And this intensified wish in turn will increase our energy for practice.

The sharp-minded practitioners begin by cultivating wisdom, which in essence is the understanding that all reality is characterized by emptiness. With such insight our admiration of the Buddha will not be based on mere faith, but will instead stem from knowledge of the causal aspects that brought about his fully enlightened state. We will thereby also recognize the subtle nature of mental afflictions and the causes that give rise to them, along with the fact that freedom from these afflictions is possible. This will lead us to realize that the essential nature of mind is simply clarity and knowing, and that the pollutants that obscure the mind are removable.

Another method for generating Bodhicitta begins with the wish that all sentient beings be free of their suffering. This leads us to assume the Bodhisattva's determination to work toward the attainment of Buddhahood in order to more effectively guide them out of their plight. According to this method, one would only proceed to cultivate wisdom—the realization of emptiness—upon having generated this determination.

While it is important to aspire to help others to any degree possible, it is essential that our practice ultimately remain aimed at the attainment of full enlightenment. We cultivate and maintain the recognition that Bodhicitta—the altruistic mind of enlightenment—is the essence of our practice, given that it is the single remedy for all woes, our own and others'. Bodhicitta is the heart of Buddhist practice; it is the most effective means for purifying negativity, the most powerful way of accumulating merit, the most skillful method for repaying the kindness of others, and will enable us to accomplish our own deepest aspirations as well as help others to do so. By means of this altruistic mind of enlightenment, we will achieve our aims for this and future lives. What's more, our practice of Bodhicitta is the greatest offering we can make to the Buddha.

As we proceed we must diligently apply countermeasures to any nonvirtuous acts we have engaged in, particularly our self-cherishing attitude. If we feel a sense of self-importance arising in us, we should immediately check it. Similarly, if we find ourselves experiencing desire for some object of attachment, our mindfulness should note this in order to quickly apply the antidote. This is how we purify our past negative acts, while also developing the vigilance by which we avoid engaging in more such acts.

We begin each day by determining to devote ourselves to our practice of Bodhicitta. We then end our day by reviewing our actions to see whether we have lived up to our aspirations; we regret our selfishly motivated actions and vow to work at not repeating them, and we rejoice in the positive ones, dedicating our virtue to the happiness of others.

MAKING USE OF DEATH

Though cultivating Bodhicitta during our lives is important, it is particularly so at the very end of life, as it is the quality of our state of mind at the time of death that determines the quality of our future rebirth. At that time we must aspire never to be parted from the altruistic mind of enlightenment. Familiarity with the death process will enable us to make constructive use of this most opportune moment.

At death the grosser aspects of consciousness cease or dissolve, revealing subtler levels of awareness. One proceeds through a series of stages, leading to what is called the clear light of death consciousness, which advanced practitioners are able to make use of to progress in their pursuit of Buddhahood. If we lack familiarity with the death process we will find the sudden experience of this most subtle level of consciousness terrifying and of no benefit. If, however, we develop familiarity with the process in daily meditation by imagining and visualizing the dissolutions that accompany death, we will not be overwhelmed by the experience when we actually undergo it. We will instead experience death with the confidence and awareness that will enable us to make productive us of it.

In preparing for the end of our lives it is helpful to give away our belongings. We do this in order to diminish our sense of attachment to things, as clinging to our possessions at the time of death is particularly harmful to the calm and contented mind-set with which we wish to face this extraordinary process. Engaging in generosity also serves to increase our store of merit. We must also purify the negative force of ill deeds, and must renew any vows and commitments we may have taken so that they will be uncompromised.

We also pray that we may never be parted from the altruistic spirit of enlightenment throughout all stages of death and beyond.

· · ·

The essence of all Buddha's teachings is aimed at countering our grasping at a sense of self and at self-cherishing thoughts. As we train our minds in virtue, strengthening our vigilance and thereby keeping self-cherishing at bay, it is not the admiration of others we rely on. It is we ourselves who best know how authentic our apparent qualities are. We proceed with courage and joy in the opportunity to develop an ideal as wondrous as Bodhicitta. This joy must be maintained as we bring this Bodhicitta into all aspects of our lives. While eating, walking down the street, or talking to our friends, the attitude of selflessly seeking full enlightenment in order to help others should enthusiastically be present. When this attitude accompanies our every physical, verbal, and mental act, we may deem ourselves trained.

Now, practice well!

CHAPTER 11

How to Practice

INTELLECTUAL UNDERSTANDING OF the path to enlightenment is important, and as discussed, a thorough grasp of emptiness is essential. But how do we translate our philosophical understanding into actual practice? We should initially reaffirm our refuge in the Three Jewels, the Buddha, the Dharma, and the Sangha. We consider the qualities of each, and commit ourselves to them. It is the Buddha who leads us along the path to freedom from the vicious cycle of misery in samsara. And it is his teachings that indicate the path we must follow. It is the advanced practitioners committed to helping others who assist us along our journey. Recollecting the qualities of each—the Buddha, the Dharma, and the Sangha—reestablishes the refuge we seek in the Three Jewels.

We also reaffirm our generation of Bodhicitta, the determination to attain the fully enlightened state of Buddhahood in order to help all sentient beings out of their suffering.

We follow this with a brief practice of accumulating virtue, purifying negativities, and enhancing our virtue through dedicating the merit we've accrued to all sentient beings.

In our practice we combine two forms of meditation: analytical meditation and calm abiding. Analytical meditation, where we reason through an idea, enables us to more powerfully affect our thoughts and emotions in order to bring about changes in our behavior. In calm abiding meditation we direct the mind on an object such as the conclusion of our analytical meditation, and keep the mind focused on that object without engaging in any contemplation or analysis. We combine these two meditative techniques by alternating between them, contemplating the logical reasoning that establishes our emptiness of inherent existence, for example, and then applying our mind to the conclusion we have reached through our analytical meditation.

When cultivating compassion, we initially contemplate the suffering that is experienced by others, by means of analytical meditation. We consider the different miserable situations in which sentient beings find themselves. We apply logical lines of reasoning to push ourselves deeper in our recognition of the subtler forms of suffering they are experiencing. When our heart is full of empathy, a strong wish to remove their suffering will arise in us. It is at this point that we focus single-pointedly and unwaveringly on this experience of compassion and refrain from further analysis. We thus alternate between the two forms of meditation in order to achieve true change in our thoughts as well as in our emotions and behavior.

The perfect meditation posture is as follows: back straight, eyes slightly closed, looking down the angle of the nose, chin slightly tucked in, legs crossed with feet over the opposite thighs, arms neither tight against the body nor sticking out, hands on lap with palms facing upward, right upon left and thumb tips touching, mouth closed, tongue lightly touching palate. This is a difficult position to comfortably maintain without long practice, and if it is too hard, sitting erect in a chair with your hands folded in your lap will suffice. However, the position of the body very definitely affects our state of mind, and it is important to assume a position that enables us to effectively maintain control of our thoughts while meditating.

We start our session by putting our preoccupations, hopes, fears, and memories aside, and bringing our mind to a neutral state. We can do this by meditating on our breath, mentally following each round of inhalation and exhalation in full, quiet awareness. Twenty such rounds of breath should enable us to bring our mind to a tranquil, neutral state. If we push ourselves to meditate before our mind has been stilled, we are likely only to increase our restlessness and frustration.

CULTIVATING WISDOM

We now direct our mind on emptiness. We begin by taking our own identity as the subject of our concentration. Repeating the thought "I am," we seek out the "I" in this sentence. What, and where, is this "I"? Though the quality of emptiness attributed to the "I" is identical to that of other phenomena, and though it is not imperative that we first meditate on the selflessness of person, it is said to be easier and more effective to begin with oneself as the object of one's emptiness meditation.

So, where is this self? Might it be the body? The mind? We carefully establish just how the self would have to exist if it did in fact exist. We then clearly establish that such a self cannot be found among the parts that make us up, nor is it to be found separate from those parts. We conclude that it therefore does not exist. Through familiarity, the nonexistence of such a self will become increasingly evident. When we look in the mirror we will immediately feel, "'I don't actually exist!'"

We then proceed to examine those things on which we base our assumption of "I." We try to locate an identity for each of them. We look for the actual body among its parts—is it our head? our chest? our arms? our legs?—and conclude that just as there is no "I" to be found among mental parts that the self is based on, so there is also no body to be found among its physical parts. When we see a reflection of our body we will be reminded instantly of its essential insubstantiality. In the same way, when we search for our mind, we reach the similar conclusion that there is no actual mind to be found among all of its constituent parts.

This is how we establish that the self exists merely as a name that we impute to its separate parts.

The effects of our analytical meditation will not be immediately evident. Through practice over time, however, as we become habituated to this new attitude toward ourselves, we will notice a change. As our understanding of emptiness deepens we will recognize the possibility, at least in principle, of attaining freedom from the entire chain of causation rooted in the fundamental ignorance that grasps at a sense of self.

ENGAGING IN METHOD

We must also meditate on the method aspect of the path to enlightenment, particularly on Bodhicitta. Meditation on Bodhicitta consists of two separate parts. We must develop the desire to bring about the welfare of all sentient beings, and we must strengthen the aim to attain Buddhahood for their benefit. It is the combination of these two aspirations that characterizes Bodhicitta.

The key to generating Bodhicitta is our cultivation of compassion. As we've discussed, we all possess a natural seed of compassion. Throughout childhood, our survival depended on the mutual affection between ourselves and our mothers. Likewise, we experienced and benefited by the affection we received from others near and dear to us. By means of analytical meditation we enhance and broaden this compassion, developing it into a feeling of sympathy for all sentient beings and a desire that they be free from all forms of suffering.

This attitude will not come about instantly, but only through diligent cultivation over many, many years. With patience and devotion, we must contemplate the state of suffering of sentient beings, and work to develop from the depths of our heart the wish that they be free of it. We start by considering the most blatant and terrible forms of suffering, then broaden our meditation to include those forms of suffering that on the surface don't appear as such. Ultimately, in order to bring about the seed of Bodhicitta we must focus on the all-pervasive suffering that comes as a result of our being conditioned by desire, aversion, and the ignorance at the core of our self-cherishing. As we contemplate how our fellow sentient beings are victims of the vicious circle of their afflicted mental states, strong revulsion will grow within us toward their afflictions and our own.

To have a true feeling of empathy toward others' pain, we begin by recognizing our own suffering and acknowledging the way we are overwhelmed by our afflictions. In our meditation we attempt to understand how our state of being is pervaded by suffering merely due to our existing within the vicious circle of samsara. We then develop the wish to free ourselves from it. Our resultant attitude is one of true renunciation. When we extend this attitude to all others and cultivate the desire that they find freedom from their suffering, compassion arises. By developing and deepening our feeling of compassion we produce the extraordinary determination, "I shall bring about the welfare of all sentient beings!" It is from this attitude that Bodhicitta arises.

Attaining Buddhahood, the goal of our meditation of Bodhicitta, will take many eons, or at least many lifetimes. We musn't expect to achieve great realizations soon, as we could thereby become discouraged in our practice. All of our efforts, even our struggle through the knottier topics we have discussed, will contribute to our enlightenment. It is therefore essential that we work to cultivate the conditions for being reborn in a situation that will enable us to continue along our path to enlightenment. By refraining from the ten nonvirtuous actions of killing, stealing, sexual misconduct, lying, divisive speech, harsh speech, idle gossip, covetousness, malice, and wrong view, we are restrained from causing others harm and from bringing about our own future suffering. This prepares us for a fortunate future life. If we are reborn as an animal we will have no opportunity to engage consciously in the practice of virtue. We must therefore nurture the short-term goal of a good rebirth that enables us to continue along our path toward the ultimate goal of Buddhahood.

At the end of our session we dedicate the merit we have accrued as a result of it, wishing that our efforts benefit all sentient beings. We can also seal our practice by again reflecting on emptiness.

Upon waking in the morning we should attempt to shape our minds. We set our motivation for the day by pledging to benefit others. I begin my day by reflecting on the qualities of the Buddha. I then pledge to give meaning to the day by devoting myself to serving others, and, at a minimum, refraining from causing them harm. I then begin my meditation as I have described above. This will positively affect my attitude for the rest of the day.

As a result of establishing our motives at the beginning of the day, when we are confronted with situations that provoke anger in us, our ability to remain patient and refrain from losing our temper will be greatly enhanced. Likewise, the shaping of our minds by our analytical meditation will enhance our ability to restrain ourselves when tempted by objects of desire, and will provide us with the inner strength necessary to avoid other afflictions such as pride and arrogance. We develop the muscle of restraint in our daily meditation session; we then manifest our inner attitudes in our daily actions.

The more of our free time we devote to shaping our minds, the better off we will be. I recommend waking up early to use the morning to meditate, especially as our mind is often at its freshest and most focused then. We must also ensure that we get sufficient sleep so that we are well rested and able to devote ourselves to our spiritual responsibilities.

We must practice consistently. We can't expect results if we only meditate sporadically. It is through the continuity of our practice that inner change will begin to take place. Although we mustn't expect to see change within days, weeks, or even months, after some years of unstinting practice, changes will definitely appear. We cannot expect any progress if we engage in our practice as a fashion, practicing for a bit and then changing to another discipline. We must practice continuously.

The idea that eons of practice are necessary to attain the full enlightenment of a Buddha is a daunting one. But when I meditate on the sheer enormity of the task before me, it actually gives me the strength to devote myself as fully as I can to serving other

sentient beings. Though such a vow may seem like wishful thinking, it can inspire us to develop confidence and to recognize that
our very existence can be of value to others. This gives meaning
to each day of our lives, infusing us with powerful courage.

THE PURPOSE OF WISDOM

The purpose of cultivating an understanding of emptiness and
meditating on emptiness is to develop a true perspective on ourselves and the world around us.

During the actual meditation on emptiness, one should be
completely absorbed in the awareness of emptiness. During
single-pointed meditation on the emptiness of "self," the meditator's mind is focused on a negative: one that doesn't affirm anything. One's consciousness is experiencing a mere negation of
any intrinsic existence of "self." In this state one faces no real
challenges. The true test of spiritual experience is faced when
we arise from this meditative absorption and engage with the
world. Sensory faculties such as sight and smell become active
again as they are exposed to external and internal conditions.
This is when our newly acquired perception of all phenomena as
illusory will serve to counter our natural tendency to grasp at a
sense of self.

Meditation on emptiness will also enable us to use adversity as a step on the path to enlightenment and experience the attitude expressed here by the Kashmiri master Shakya Sri: "When happy may I dedicate my happiness to all, and when suffering may the ocean of misery dry up." For someone who is truly able to practice Dharma in this way, living in the heart of New York City is more effective than being sequestered away on a mountaintop. If we have not developed the required inner peace, then even if we are living the life of a hermit, our minds will be overwhelmed with anger and hatred, and we will have no peace.

As Shantideva encourages us in his *Guide to the Bodhisattva's Way of Life*, we should work to "Overcome all forms of weariness and ride the horse of Bodhicitta, traveling from place of joy to place of joy. What intelligent person wouldn't delight in such a journey?"

AFTERWORD

MANY YEARS AGO, I was fortunate enough to ask His Holiness the Dalai Lama what was the most important teaching of the Buddha. He was silent for a moment. "*Shunya*," he said. "Emptiness." In my own experience, the teachings of the Buddha are of vast benefit to us. Like effective medicine, they address our own personal issues in a very specific way. And of course they share striking resonances with teachers and teachings of other spiritual paths. Love, compassion, charity, honesty, kindness, generosity, altruism, joy, and forgiveness are qualities most—if not all—beings recognize and admire. Buddhism puts great emphasis on developing these wonderful qualities to their fullest.

But Shakyamuni Buddha's great and unique gift to us was to explain the root cause of all our problems, individually as well as in our communities and nations. That cause is an unchallenged belief in an independent, eternal self. We suffer and behave badly because we believe we exist the way we appear to exist, powered from our own side, independent and real.

The Buddha suggested that this was a hallucination, a lie that ultimately has led to all our problems and suffering since beginningless time. We are so habituated to—so saturated with—this falsehood that we only see glimmers of the truth with enormous and sustained effort and with the kind help of those who have seen through the hallucination themselves.

As an actor and filmmaker, I'm amazed at my own willingness to suspend my disbelief when watching a movie. Clearly, I know there isn't literally anything there but light and shadow projected at twenty-four frames a second on a flat white screen. It's a magic trick created by filmmaker magicians. Still I can get caught up in my own tricks. The movie we experience is a convention, a language of storytelling that we willingly accept. Our minds do the rest: filling in the blanks, creating the illusion of solid reality, movement, and continuity. On the basis of our willingness to commit ourselves to the illusion as *real*, we generate emotions. We *love* the heroes. We *hate* the villains. We *fear* the monsters. We *weep* with joy or with sorrow. We are transported. This sense of reality is confirmed by the flow of our emotions.

The lights come up and we "wake up" to conventional reality

and can discuss with a degree of mirth and detachment, admiration or disdain, the two-hour movie reality we've been carried away by. The magic spell is broken. But still something remains.

Perhaps our short lives are metaphorically the same. We give ourselves to the experience of life as real, trusting that our senses, thoughts, and emotions are real simply because we experience them.

From a Buddhist point of view, the surface of things may not be so reliable. Even the idea of a self is questioned. And Buddhism suggests that's all it is—an idea. That "out there" is deeply connected to "in here" in ways we've probably never considered. We experience "out there" not as *it is*, but as *we are*. Our world and our experience of it is projected on the white screen of consciousness. It's a story.

It's said that the Buddha's final teaching to his disciples was to "tame your minds," which also implies to "*train* your minds," meaning that after having slowed the constant chatter of the mind and loosened the obsessive nature of our belief in a permanent self, one can then *train* one's mind to see with clarity and insight the true nature of mind itself. This true nature is emptiness.

Everything, self and phenomena, all we experience, even emptiness itself, is empty of inherent existence. The Buddha didn't suggest that self, other, and phenomena don't exist. They do. They simply don't exist the way they *appear* to exist. Every-thing exists interdependently, in a constant flow of becoming, changing, and transforming. If that is the case, then ultimately the only thing to embrace with conviction is the pure essence of the mind itself. This is emptiness: the pure screen that the world and the story of self is projected on.

When I was in my early twenties, having first seriously en-gaged Buddhism, the concept of emptiness suggested to me a vague kind of oblivion. I thought that if I were able to achieve Shunya, I would literally disappear. No more me, therefore no more me to suffer. It was a negation of life itself, and, of course, quite silly. But it's vitally important to know who we are . . . and what the world is. We need a correct and consistent view that will keep us on track.

But emptiness is not a concept. It's not an idea. It's the way things are. It has no center and no boundaries. It is not static. It can't be found in conventional language. Great poetry might point us in the right direction. But the great white whale a Bud-dhist seeks is Buddhahood—a complete awakening from limita-tion, a complete awakening from the hallucination of an eternal, independent self. And it can be achieved only through a motiva-tion of selfless compassion for all beings without exception.

A genuine experience of emptiness is like a sighting of the

great white whale. Courage, wisdom, determination, and great compassion are our harpoons.

But none of this is easy. After almost forty years of practice and hundreds of teachings from incredibly patient teachers, the whale is still elusive.

What I can say is that with even the beginnings of an intellectual understanding of emptiness, the meditative practices on the development of both wisdom and compassion become richer and more productive. A certain taste starts to arise, a certain confidence that the goal is possible. One's nature becomes softer and the afflictive emotions loosen their hold.

I recently bought my son a new baseball glove. He had outgrown his first one. He had to choose between two perfectly good ones. He chose the glove that was harder to break in, the one he couldn't use immediately because the leather was thicker and stiffer. It would need more work and attention. But as the expert told us, in the end this would be the better glove for him, and would last longer. So for days now we have been rubbing the special oils into it, working it, bringing it to life. And it has slowly been loosening up and becoming pliable. And it will continue to get better the more he uses it.

The same is true with His Holiness's teachings. None of this is easy. It all takes effort. The Buddha himself almost died with the effort. But the rewards are great. Beyond measure. I find it incredibly moving that these great beings like His Holiness the Dalai Lama still do the heavy lifting, still do the hard work on themselves every day, all day. Even with the vast wisdom and compassion His Holiness has generated over countless life-times, still he arises from sleep each day at three thirty a.m. to set his altruistic motivation and begin his hours of practices before engaging in another full day of being of benefit to others. What an inspiration!

My dear friend and teacher Khyongla Rato Rinpoche and I are deeply grateful to His Holiness for his kindness and patience in giving these extraordinary teachings to us. And of course to my trusted partner Venerable Nicholas Vreeland for compiling them into this fine book.

May it be of joyous benefit to all beings. May we all achieve happiness and the causes of the supreme happiness, Buddhahood.

Richard Gere